Surviving Death
  What Loss Taught Me About Love, Joy, and Meaning

By Kate O'Neill

Copyright © 2015 by Kate O'Neill
First Edition, 2015

Published in the United States of America

Disclaimer

The stories and ideas contained in this book are based on my own personal experiences and are shared only for educational purposes and to raise awareness of social issues around grief and loss. Nothing in this book is intended to be a substitute for psychological or medical care based on your specific circumstances and needs.

If you believe you might need help coping with loss, I would lovingly encourage you to seek it. In particular, within the U.S., the National Suicide Prevention Lifeline is (800) 273-TALK (8255). An international directory of suicide hotlines can be found at
http://www.iasp.info/resources/Crisis_Centres/.

Be well.

Acknowledgements

I don't know how to begin to acknowledge the many people who have some hand in helping me write this book. So much of what made it possible was in the form of support and encouragement.

But a special thank you must go to Robbie Quinn, my photographer and fiancé, whose work I use on the cover and "About the Author" page, and without whose gentle encouragement I might never have finished.

Dedication

To My Girls:
especially Jen, Ashley, Tara, Paige,
and the High-Heelers

"The death of someone we know always reminds us that we are still alive — perhaps for some purpose which we ought to re-examine."
— Mignon McLaughlin

"A man's dying is more the survivors' affair than his own."
— Thomas Mann

CHAPTER ONE

INTRODUCTION

A Fuller Picture of Life After Loss

If you're reading this, you've probably lost someone close to you, and the first thing I want to say to you is that I'm so very sorry for your loss.

The next thing I want to say to you is that I sincerely hope the stories I share in this book describe the grief process in a way that might bring you some comfort and hope.

After my husband died in 2012, quite a few friends gave me books on coping with grief and loss. They all offered *something* of value, even the ones that were decades old and full of dated and somewhat ludicrous ideas about what it means to be a widow in society. But what I never found were stories that resonated with the fullness of how complex my feelings were: lonely, dark, anguished, broken, and frightened, and yet simultaneously full of expansive gratitude, tentative hope, deepened purpose, and passionate appreciation of the joy and love I have had in my life.

It seemed that in dealing with the delicate subject of death and loss, few writers had examined the overshadowed but nonetheless important gifts that come with the blow of surviving the loss of someone you loved so much: the friendship and love you may find yourself surrounded with, the meaning and joy you might seek, and the strength you might recognize in yourself at merely surviving it all.

I was incredibly fortunate to have a gracious and generous group of friends who supported me, and even on the first day of the greatest loss of my life thus far, gratitude for their actions swelled in me like I'd never before experienced. That feeling was my clue that the mechanics of grief as I'd heard them before, and even as I'd previously experienced myself with the loss of my father seven years before, weren't going to apply to me in this case, and that perhaps other people were also surviving death by embracing the love still around them, using their expanded perspective to recognize opportunities to live a richer and more meaningful life.

During the first few years after my dad died and after my husband died, I blogged, kept extensive journals, posted updates online, and wrote emails and notes to friends, and sometimes these thoughts seemed to capture an element of the process in a way I hoped might help others coping with loss.

So I've collected and arranged some of my personal stories, reflections, and thoughts on the process at various stages to share with you here.

Some of these stories do explore the moments of darkness and despair, but a good deal more of what I've written looks for light. That seems to be my predisposition in life. If it is yours, too, then I suspect you may find yourself agreeing or smiling or in some way relating to many of my observations, be they warped or wise. But even if you are not normally inclined to find the best in every situation, and perhaps especially if you're not inclined that way, I hope that some of what I've shared here may be valuable to you in some way. I certainly never intend to diminish the importance of the people I've lost from my life or that you've lost from yours by not dwelling on my sadness at losing them; on the contrary, I hope to honor them by living as full and true a life as I can achieve.

My hope is that by adding to the grays and blacks of our usual discussions of grief and mourning with some vibrant colors and spikes of joy and love, that perhaps we can see start to see life-altering loss as a passage into renewed purpose and clarity, and begin to rebuild our futures more fully and with more meaning.

Who Is This Book For: A Note on the Roles of Grief

I set out to write something that would be helpful for the people who were like me when my husband died: the closest person to the person who had died. The one who had, in a sense, most *survived* the death.

But I also realized that the people around me were grieving, and that they still stepped up to support me. There were things they did that might be helpful guidance to someone who feels sad and helpless and wants to know what they can do. So I'm writing to the friends and family, too — really, *everyone* who has experienced that loss.

When someone dies, many, many people might be affected. Of course we expect grief from the spouses and parents and children and other immediate family, the very close friends, and so on. The concentric rings of effect expand out from there: social friends, coworkers, neighbors, friends from churches and clubs, faraway friends, former lovers, and even, perhaps, the waiter at the restaurant where the deceased was a regular. We can never underestimate the impact we have on the people we encounter, and how our loss will reverberate throughout our chosen communities.

For these people on the outer perimeters of acquaintance, their interactions with the person who has died may have been brief and their loss may seem trivial to the people who were closer. But grief has a way of amplifying our feelings, and those who had only passing conversations may now attach tremendous significance to those interactions.

The key, it seems, to community healing is for us all to recognize our relative role to the person who died, and to share the burden of grief proportionately. The person or people who were closest are going to be nearly overwhelmed with grief, and how others share their grief will either help them feel less alone or burden them with an additional sense of responsibility. The approach that makes the most sense to me was described perfectly by Susan Silk and Barry Goldman in an April 2013 article in the Los Angeles Times called "How Not to Say the Wrong Thing," and it has been summarized since as "Comfort In; Dump Out." It's a bit of an oversimplification, but generally, the rule is that the people who are closer may grieve and lament and complain to the people who are less close, and the people who are less close may listen and sympathize and support. The approach works because there is always someone who is less close, so anyone at any distance from the closest griever who may be feeling grief has an outlet, whether that's a therapist or even a kind stranger. But that outlet should probably not be a person who is feeling an even more acute sense of loss.

Other Ways to Think and Feel About Loss

You may already be familiar, as I was before experiencing significant loss, with the pervasive idea that grief occurs in five stages: denial, anger, bargaining, depression, and acceptance. These are the stages of the Kübler-Ross model, named after Elisabeth Kübler-Ross who developed it. What I didn't know was that she was actually describing the stages that patients go through when they have a terminal illness. These stages are describing the process of dying, not the process of surviving death.

Still, the reason I suspect they are so popularly cited is that they are close enough to what the bereaved experience to be helpful, and no other model is nearly as commonly known.

What I found, though, was that these stages didn't do justice to what I experienced, and I wanted to describe the process better. I made notes when my mind was up to it and talked with other grievers. I may still have missed a few but I did observe some stages the Kübler-Ross model leaves out. They don't cancel out the other stages; they just seemed to augment them. Just like the Kübler-Ross stages, they don't happen sequentially; they were a little all over the place.

So what I submit are some additional aspects of grief that I don't think we recognize socially as much as we could and maybe should, and which you may or may not experience yourself after a profound loss:

Shock (As Opposed to Denial)

The first moments felt surreal. Almost like being in a movie. But I don't recognize them as having been *denial*, per se. As I recall, I accepted the reality of the situation, just in graduating stages that made it increasingly clearer what the consequences of that reality were.

The word and the idea of "denial" as the accepted first stage of grief sets up an expectation that you are living in la-la land, and that people around you aren't sure you know what's really going on, whereas you very well may know and understand better than anyone what's really going on. The word "shock" better communicates the likelihood that you're present in the moment, but overwhelmed by everything you know has changed, and your processing system is just overloaded.

Denial is real, and I'm not suggesting that some people don't go through it as part of their process, and while it could be a healthy part of the process for those people, I don't think it's a healthy *expectation* to have overall, either for the closest griever or for those assisting him or her.

Overwhelm and Leaning on Those Around You

The recurring theme of the initial stages seems to be "overwhelmed." There is so much that immediately needs doing and processing once someone dies, that without the help of friends or family who will truly step up and assist, that burden will add tremendously to the difficulty of dealing with the reality at hand.

I remember repeatedly saying "I just wish I knew what I should be doing" and my friends assuring me that I didn't need to *do* anything. That's about as well as the situation can go.

Gratitude

There's so much to say about gratitude. I don't know how it came to be the most important component of my grief, but it did, and I'm even grateful for that. I felt grateful to the friends who showed up to help, grateful for the time and love I'd had with my husband that allowed me to appreciate what we had before he died, grateful for the fact that my father's death seven years prior had taught me a little of what to expect, and so on. Feeling grateful was somehow an easy outlet for my sadness, and I felt it constantly.

Letting the Finality Sink In

Not quite denial and not quite acceptance, there is the layered understanding of what this new reality means. Just because you acknowledge the death of someone close to you doesn't mean that it has occurred to you all at once how many ways you will be reminded of their absence, and how many parts of your life will be affected.

This is an area where slow, gradual deaths from chronic illness, with their "pre-grief" awareness, differ significantly for the grieving community from sudden deaths. It's going to take time in either case to grasp the impact of the loss; it's just that sometimes that time happens partially before the actual death takes place, and sometimes it all can only begin after. I would never suggest one is somehow easier or harder; having lost my father slowly and my husband suddenly, I know that both are complex. But it may help to know what's happening as you're processing the reality in either case.

Rebuilding and Trying It Out

There are important tasks to be done and milestones to achieve before getting back to work, getting back to social life, and trying to resume or rebuild your life. Some people get right back into their routines, and hey, if that's the thing that helps you survive, I'm not here to judge. But when people experienced devastating loss, they often get a new perspective on life and a new sense of what matters. It seems like a terrible thing to waste by not using that perspective to assess what you want to (or perhaps need to) keep constant from your old life, what you might allow yourself to abandon, and what you want to recreate in a new way.

When you do start going back to work, going out with friends, or generally being in the mix of normal life, it can be incredibly hard to be surrounded both by people who know what's happened and who may ask questions that unsettle you, as well as people who don't know and will treat you indifferently. And then there are the people whose well-meaning but over-the-top interaction with you reduces you to a tragic figure rather than a person who is coming through loss with dignity and strength. You'll need your energy, and possibly a friend to help deflect overly personal questions, but it can be done.

Seeking Joy and Laughter

The most bittersweet stage, perhaps, is recognizing that life is not over for you, and you might like to laugh, love, and feel joy. It can seem impossible in the very first moments of loss, but even in the early days, there may be moments of laughter when you and your surviving loved ones reminisce. Sometimes, if your sense of humor is a little twisted like mine is, you may be quietly amused at our collective social absurdity and awkwardness around death and grief. And eventually you'll likely feel the pull towards chances to enjoy life again and have more happy moments. It's a good instinct. Society can sometimes seem to want to shame us for seeking laughter, love, and joy after loss, and, probably due to larger social inequalities around gender, that shaming seems particularly acute for widows. But that's a facet of how we deal with death that needs to evolve: by no means should we downplay the importance of the dead, but by all means, we should appreciate and support the living.

Seeking and Creating Meaning in Life

In the longest stage after loss — the rest of your life — the opportunity exists for meaningful interactions, meaningful direction in life, and meaning at every level. You can evaluate everything you do and see through a new lens: what really matters. It's a profound opportunity to live a more full life and in so doing, to also honor your lost loved one.

Whether you experience the Kübler-Ross stages *and* these stages, or some other combination of stages, the most important thing to recognize about grief is to understand and believe that whatever you're feeling is valid and real. If you need help, please get it. I did, and I'm glad I did. I hope you do what's right for you.

A Note About the Rest of This Book

Just as I wrote that the stages don't necessarily occur in sequence, I didn't want this book to follow these stages or this sequence too closely so as not to suggest that there is only one right way and one right order. And I didn't think that presenting the stories chronologically would create the sense that there is some pattern to the feelings we may experience during grief. Instead, I chose to write this book as a collection of stories and personal reflections loosely grouped by feeling and focusing on what most helped me find joy and meaning. I sincerely hope that somehow, something in these stories helps you, too.

CHAPTER TWO

GRATITUDE

The Link Between Gratitude and Hope

Nashville, TN
November 27, 2013.

For a while now, I've been working on two books: one is a methodology for marketing with meaning, and one is a sort of memoir on grief and meaning. This one.

Writing two books at once might seem crazy, but it feels kind of natural, actually. They cover such different ground that I can write in almost any headspace and be making progress on one or the other. I've been joking with friends that I've discovered "productive procrastination," but it's true, actually: writing a book at all is a tremendously disciplined exercise, so having a second book to fall back on as an escape from the other helps keep the wheels moving and the writing muscle strong.

Anyway, I say all this to say it's hard. I don't mean that in a whiny way, but in a "wow, I'm so glad I'm forcing myself to do this" kind of way. I'm grateful for the intellectual and emotional challenge that each of these books is making me rise up to. It's odd, because since Karsten died, I feel like I've been capable of deeper, more expansive, and more connected thinking, but less focus. I hope it gets easier but the work seems healthy, and I'm grateful.

And actually, that's a topic I've been exploring in my work, which is timely, what with it being Thanksgiving week: the nature of gratitude and of hope.

I've been digging into how the day Karsten died, my friend Ashley led me and a group of my first-responder friends through a deep breathing exercise, and she suggested we each think of a word and focus on it. On that day, of all days, without conscious correction, the word I focused on as we breathed in was "gratitude." And it turned out that was the word my friend Jen chose, too.

I think at first glance, gratitude and hope might seem to be at odds with one another. Because if you are truly grateful for what you have, you should have no need to hope for better, right? But I don't think that's how gratitude really works in practice. Because gratitude isn't about pretending that awful things don't happen. Gratitude does not mean denial. Shitty things happen, and people are sometimes shortsighted or petty or downright cruel, and sometimes you are going to be lonely or sad or angry or scared. And yet you can still be grateful. And you can still have hope.

Because I think what a mindset of gratitude is about is not letting yourself get stuck. Gratitude means recognizing reality with all its flaws and saying OK, that's how things are. You might have to get pretty creative about what you're grateful for. You might have to get pretty creative about what you're hopeful about. Whether you have to look to the past or the future, whether you have to confront people's flaws or embrace their virtues in spite of them, whatever you have to do, it's about finding a way to move things forward. Because every day you're alive you can still hope for better, and that in itself is something to be grateful for.

The Thank-You Cards

Matteson, IL
    August 2005.

* * *

I'd been standing in the greeting card aisle at Target for twenty minutes, searching for something that basically said "now that I'm dying, I want to thank you for a lifetime of friendship." My dad had asked me the day before to help him write thank-you notes. Actually, he'd asked me to help him write "sympathy cards," but he realized his mistake and got flustered trying to correct himself and couldn't think of the words for "thank-you notes." Regardless, I had immediately understood my assignment, and the significance of it. But now it seemed that all the thank-you cards were almost cruelly consistent in their lightness and fluffiness. My weight was shifting from side to side, and I realized that my eyes were glazing over. I reluctantly concluded that Hallmark didn't make the exact card I wanted. Or if they did, it wasn't filed neatly under a handy category like the "Birthday - Him" cards were. Or even the "Sympathy" cards. I smirked, wondering what the category would be called. "Thanks - From Dying Friend"?

Karsten, my husband, often commented on my dark sense of humor, and how he could tell things were bad for me when I was really funny. He was at that moment standing in the opposite aisle, facing me across the display rack, trying to help me search but having as little success as I was. I could see enough of his face through the opening in the shelves between us to see his furrowed brow as he picked up card after card, reading and putting each one back in its place.

Eventually I found a few cards with life-affirming quotations from dead poets inscribed on the front and nothing printed inside. I bought all of them.

All day, I looked for an opening to sit with my dad and take his dictation. He was terribly weak, though, and unable or unwilling to speak. He'd been diagnosed with malignant metastatic melanoma two years prior, and since then the cancer had spread to his lymph nodes, his liver, his lungs, and most recently, to his brain. The first time he was given a week to live had been at least six months before, and again at least eight times since then. For a while, it had become a darkly comic shared experience for my mom, my sister, my husband, and me each time the doctors solemnly told us that he probably only had a week to live. But now he hadn't been out of his bed in weeks and was barely eating. Late in the afternoon, when I thought he seemed more energetic, I asked him if he wanted to write the notes, but he shook his head.

Karsten and I had planned to leave early the next morning to drive back to Nashville, so I was feeling a sense of urgency.

It was now August, and we'd been driving back and forth between Chicago and Nashville for the better part of a year, initially spending a few days in Chicago to be present for my dad's treatments, followed by a few weeks at home, trying to catch up on work, renovating the historic home we'd bought in March, spending quality time with our six cats, and basically trying to maintain as normal a life as possible in the face of my father's imminent death. ("Normal life" was made even more remote by the surprising loss of Karsten's mother in the spring.) But as my dad's illness progressed through the spring and summer, that schedule reversed and we would spend a week or more in Chicago, driving back to Nashville for just long enough to check in on our cats, do laundry, and turn around to head back to help with caring for my dad and do whatever my mom needed to help her cope with losing him.

As it turned out, it wasn't until the morning after I bought the cards, at almost precisely the moment when Karsten and I had planned to leave, that my dad seemed ready. I tried asking him fifty different ways what he wanted to say, and he was silent each time. But his face said volumes, so I gently suggested that I write the notes from my perspective, sitting at his bedside, and let the recipients know what I thought he might be trying to tell them. He liked that idea, so I came up with a basic formula and ran it by him, and got a teary-eyed nod of approval.

I tweaked and customized it for different recipients, but the basic formula went like this:

Dear (recipient)
Yesterday morning, my father asked me to help him write a thank you note to you.

This morning, I sat down with him to transcribe his message, and that proved a harder task than imagined. I am writing to you from his bedside, and what I see in his face as he struggles to find the words is gratitude. What he seems to want to say is thank you for everything - your support, your kindness, your prayers, and most of all, your love.

I hope you know the importance you've had in my father's life, and how much he appreciates you. And for that, our whole family appreciates you, too.

(signed by me and by my dad)

I wrote them all out, and hoped it would do the job. And then Karsten and I set out together for home.

The Bothness of It

Nashville, TN
November 2013.

It probably makes me sound like a nerd and possibly like an addict, but occasionally during that first day after Karsten died and more frequently the next day, I thought about Facebook.

It's just that I'd heard from friends that people were posting about it, about the fact that Karsten had died, and about how sad they were for me, about how much of a loss his death was, and even about how they didn't know what had happened. I knew there was a community of people who communicated primarily through digital media who were out there, you know, communicating. And I wanted to see it, read it, feel the sharing of it, be part of it, bathe in it. If I couldn't have Karsten, I felt, I wanted to bask in the love of Karsten in whatever form it was available.

What sold me was a blog post from a friend who did a particularly eloquent job of talking about the phenomenon of closeness. When my friend Joel died in college, I observed the way people attached themselves to his memory as if they'd been close, and I struggled to understand it. On one hand, it was very easy to feel compassion for people who may have felt regret that they weren't closer, or who may have felt an awakening of their own sense of mortality. But on the other, less generous, hand, it struck me as a kind of morbid scene-stealing, or a desperate attempt to be part of something that seemed important.

What my friend wrote in that blog post was about how people seemed surprised that he knew Karsten, because Karsten seemed kind of weird. And people asked this friend if they were close. So he mused on what it means to be close. And he ultimately answered the people asking him by saying they were "close enough."

Reading that blog post inspired me. I felt more encouraged in the idea that it was possible to be emotionally honest about grief and loss without being overly dramatic. I felt tremendous gratitude for him in writing that post.

And I felt the need to write something, even if it was just a post to Facebook.

So that night around 3 AM, after nearly 48 hours and a whole lot of death-related activity and decision-making, I posted an update to my wall.

Tuesday, June 26, 2012 at 3:15am CDT
Kate O'Neill updated her status.
Three AM is a lonely time of night, but I'm using

this time to review the lovely, sympathetic, supportive things many of you have said in the wake of Karsten's passing. Yesterday Ashley led me and a group of my awesome first-responder friends through a deep breathing exercise and the word I focused on as we breathed in was "gratitude" — which you have made so much more real by simply being an amazing community. Thank you. I treasure you all.

It turned out, of course, that this was to be the message by which many of my more distant friends found out that Karsten had died. That possibility had occurred to me when writing it, and I decided to focus on my own feelings and the people around me instead of Karsten, as a way of softening the blow.

When I blogged about it the next morning, I had the same awareness that this was a kind of press release to the distant friends and acquaintances who hadn't yet heard the news, and a kind of status report to those who had.

Nashville, TN
June 2012.

The human condition, I suppose, is to be capable of deep, thorough, feel-it-ache-in-your-bones love, and to be mortal anyway, and know you'll someday lose it, one way or the other. It is, inevitably, not fair.

❊ ❊ ❊

My partner/husband/best friend/co-conspirator/
co-writer/better half/true love of my life, Karsten
Soltauer, left us Monday morning. But he also
left behind a body of artwork that speaks even
more loudly now that he has lost his beautiful
voice.

His voice.
I used to love talking with Karsten on the phone.
I'd call him from the car on my drive home, even
though my office is only about a mile away,
because it gave me a few minutes to hear his
voice on the phone. It was so sexy and soothing. I
wish I had a recording of him telling me he loved
me forever, as he did many times each day.

Before we met, he'd experienced a loss of his
own: his ex-girlfriend of nearly eight years had
left him about a year prior, and he was nursing a
broken heart. He channeled that pain into
working through a series of marbled paper
found-image pieces. Karsten spent 80 hours per
piece studying the random curls of color, shading

the contours of the swirled patterns to reveal images. Like watching clouds for shapes, but then tracing them with marker into the sky so other people could see what he saw.

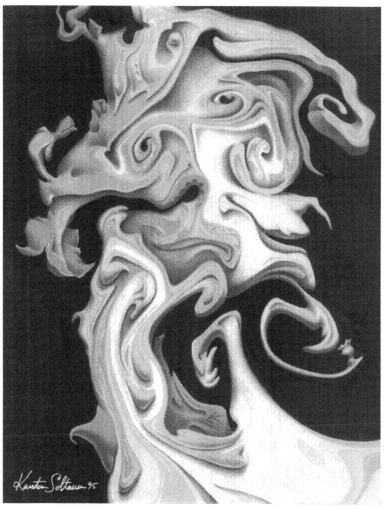

One of Karsten's "swirly" pieces

from the "Curvature of the Mind" series

Despite many, many experiments with style, form, and media, this was the central theme of Karsten's life-long artistic vision: finding what no one else would have spotted, or bothered to look for.

I think perhaps the key to processing a loss this immense and intense is to embrace the bothness of it: I have never experienced one emotion without the potential for its complement. I am nowhere near the master observer of absurdity that Karsten was, but I have been his student for nearly fifteen years and maybe I can see it a bit more than most. But if devastating loss is a swing to the left from the emotional equilibrium, I sense there is the opening of an often unnoticed rather large area to the right, into gratitude, appreciation, abundance, humor, and moments of joy and peace.

Like Karsten's "Curvature of the Mind" series, as he later named the swirling marbled pieces, there are treasures to be found in the chaos. You just have to really look for them. And pencil stroke by pencil stroke, you shade out what doesn't contribute to the picture you want to remain. But the bothness of it is that just as the oil and water needed to be mixed to make the paper, and the darker shadowing needs to be drawn in to see the colorful image more clearly, so do the dark emotions bring contrast to the lighter ones, and we can seek those out if we choose to. At least, that's my hope.

CHAPTER THREE

FORWARD MOTION

Mixed Metaphors, and Life After Death

Nashville, TN
  November 4, 2012.

You might not know it by the fact that I've written so much about grief, but I really can be a whole lot of fun. I think about many topics besides death. I laugh far, far more often than I cry. And I smile most of the time; I just do. But almost invariably, the moments that seem to merit deeper examination in writing are those when I'm pulling together my thoughts about life in a big picture sense. And the thing about life is, death is what puts it in sharpest perspective.

So excuse my dwelling on the subject, but I've got life after death on my mind. Not the eternal kind, shrouded in uncertainty, but the unquestionable way your own life continues after someone you love dies. It's on my mind because tomorrow it will have been seven years since my dad died.

I realize what a challenging thing this is to try to articulate, but ever since Karsten's death, one of the many things I've found myself feeling grateful for is that I had some experience coping with significant loss already. Obviously I'm not in any way saying that I'm grateful that my dad died; just that if those events—losing my father and losing my husband—had to happen in my life, that at least the ordering of them feels somehow merciful. When Karsten died, I had the beginnings of an idea of what to expect from grief and how it would feel as I tried to move forward once the initial shock had cleared.

I find myself thinking and talking a lot about the idea of forward motion, because there's this fairly intuitive way in which recovery and healing is like a journey. But the experience is dimensional in ways that one metaphor doesn't adequately describe. So I also find myself thinking and talking about regrowth. In the last blog post I wrote here, "On choosing what to keep ," I mentioned how I read from the poem "In Blackwater Woods" at my dad's funeral and I quoted the last few lines of that poem, about loving deeply and letting go, which are the lines that run through my head most often. But the poem also starts with imagery about fall and the turning leaves, and brings to mind how everything in nature moves cyclically toward a kind of death with only a vague notion of the idea of "salvation." Spring and regrowth, which may be what "salvation" really is, seem abstract and far-off as the days get shorter and colder and everything seems bare and exposed.

And here we are with the leaves turning around us, and the days getting shorter and colder, and everything seeming exposed, and spring seeming far away. But regrowth in nature isn't really as abstract as the concept of salvation. It's just that in winter, growth is sometimes happening where you can't see it.

After seven years of missing my dad and learning what grief means in the long run, I know there's no rushing regrowth. But I also know how much happens under the surface, and how strong I've become and am still becoming in ways few people can see.

There's another metaphor to add to this already convoluted mix, too. It's a story I've been telling a few close friends to try to explain my state of mind, and it goes like this: in the late '90s, when I was working in my first Silicon Valley startup, I had a coworker named Rick who was really into physics. One day, a group of coworkers were out for a team lunch in a restaurant with paper placemats and crayons, and while we waited for our food I started doodling. I've always had a fondness for art that incorporates words and imagery, so whenever I draw anything, even for a goof, I tend to listen for a phrase that seems meaningful. I don't remember what it was about physics that Rick was describing, but at some point he jokingly summarized whatever he was saying with "they expanded space, but compressed time, so it was OK." I immediately wrote those words around the outside of my placemat and drew some kind of visual interpretation of that concept. I had no idea why I was so attracted to it, but somehow it stuck with me all these years.

The way I think of it now, when you face the reality of death, you simultaneously confront the certainty of mortality, the enormity of all life, the insignificance of our lifespan in the overall continuum of time, and the myopia of our usual moment-by-moment perspective. Suddenly, the horizon looks wider, there is more depth to all experience, and everything—everything—seems both more trivial and more urgent. In other words, space expands, and time compresses. And it is OK.

At least for a while. Like I said, having been through life after death before, I know that eventually that perspective readjusts: the horizon narrows a little, and the feeling that life is so, so short begins to subside just enough.

That readjustment doesn't just take time, though, despite what conventional wisdom might have you believe. It takes a bit of practice, and deliberately exposing yourself to the vastness of the reality so that you can strengthen your stride for the forward motion. I know what I did there, but it really does take all those metaphors just to come close to describing the process as I see it.

And I'm really motivated to describe it. Not just for myself, but for other people who may—will—eventually face life after death. I don't think we, culturally or socially, do a very good job of preparing people for it. There's work involved, and some new ways of seeing things.

As an insight into my own process, I will share that I have a Spotify playlist called "musical therapy" with a bunch of songs that I strongly associate with Karsten. I listened to it while I was in the shower this morning, cried some, and then sat down and wrote a song about memories, what you keep as you move forward, and what you really can let go of. And now I'm smiling and feeling strong and healthy. I miss my dad, I miss Karsten, and the healing has been hard work, but I'm clearly both moving forward and regrowing. I don't care if I'm mixing metaphors; the horizon is still pretty wide, and there's room enough to see it a few different ways.

Life Goes On

Chicago, IL
August 10, 2013.

I'm back in Chicago this weekend, celebrating my great nephew's 3rd birthday. I haven't seen him in quite a few months; he's grown so much and he speaks short phrases in both English and Spanish. A lot about him has changed since I last saw him.

When I spend time with my family, I get the acute sense of the passage of time. In my own life it's both because I am so easily reminded of both my dad and Karsten, but also because I know that I've grown so much and a lot about me has changed since they last saw me.

The thing about the phrase "life goes on" is that when people say it, it's supposed to paint this reassuring picture of continuity and solidity that relaxes you. But what isn't communicated by that phrase is that on one hand, there's a part of the process where life going on as if nothing has happened is the most absurd, unsettling thing you can experience. And on the other hand, life is never exactly the same after significant loss, so continuity is somewhat meaningless.

I don't mean that in a despairing way. In many ways, the fact that life is never really the same is good: once you have experienced significant loss, you have the chance to live with an awareness of life that you might otherwise have missed. Having lost both my father and my husband in my 30s, I have a deepened, clearer perspective and a well of strength from which to live my 40s through the rest of my life, which I hope is long and healthy and happy.

Life goes on. When my dad died, I struggled returning to work for a variety of reasons, one of them being that I was having a hard time interacting with people whose foundation hadn't just been shaken. Perhaps the best that can be said about going through difficult times is that, if we allow ourselves, we can become better listeners, more empathetic, more in touch with our deepest hopes and fears, and more aware and appreciative of the precious fleeting goodness all around us. That awareness feels both good and bad. It's hard to function normally in society when you're a walking barometer of other people's emotional states. Maybe that's a version of being made "stronger" by that which does not kill you, but it's certainly not the kind of "stronger" I was ever anticipating.

Life goes on. I eventually quit my job and went elsewhere. The next few years were a progression of jobs, all of which were interesting, some of which were fulfilling, but all of which left me feeling like I needed something more. Four years later, I started my own company, and the next few years were tough but rewarding. And *then*: my husband died. And work became a struggle again. My focus was again shattered and dispersed to that weird kind of "stronger," and I knew I wasn't doing what I wanted to be doing. After a year and a half of trying to recover and regain my enthusiasm for my business, I decided it was time to move on.

Life does go on. Time is indifferent, nature is consistent, and everything looks exactly the same in ways that seem like they should have changed, and at the same time your surroundings have been upended and everything looks completely different in ways you never expect.

Life goes on. And as long as we know what that *really means*, as long as the idea of it isn't lulling us into a sense of complacency and mediocrity, as long as we can make peace with both the chaos and the rhythm of life, we go on, too, and we can rebuild and reinvent and ultimately thrive and maybe surprise our loved ones when they see us again and notice how much we've grown.

Adversity and Forward Motion

Nashville, TN
  March 15, 2014.

It seems only natural after you lose someone to suicide to reflect on what caused them anguish, what adversity they struggled with, and how, and for how long. And when I think about the kinds of adversity Karsten and I went through together, it's a hell of a long list, spanning emotional traumas, financial setbacks, and situational difficulties of all kinds.

There were the deaths, of course, of three of our parents, several of our friends, and one of our cats. There were countless financial challenges throughout the years, a few hardships, and many moments of uncertainty. Creative blocks and artistic difficulties. A hard drive crash and months of songwriting work lost. We moved long distance enough times that there were boxes we never unpacked. We bought a historic house that would make most "fixer-uppers" look like an afternoon project, and he took on the vast majority of the work himself. We dealt with rats, fleas, roaches, and a city-wide flood of historic proportions. He lost art in the flood, and supplies, and a workspace he'd just built. There were the challenges of my work, although I learned not to bring them home with me. Still, I worked too long; he worked too hard. He questioned himself, questioned his questioning of himself, questioned why I had such unquestioning love for him. And all of this happened in under fifteen years.

The strain of all that adversity took a toll on both of us, but for whatever reason — the genetic lottery of brain chemistry, perhaps — we both managed it and even hid it in our own ways. What adversity did for me, eventually, was toughen me. Stiffen my resolve. I knew I'd been through X and survived, so X didn't really terrify me anymore. What happened for Karsten was the opposite. He'd been through X and it nearly destroyed him, and he believed — no, I suppose he *knew* — that he couldn't survive X again.

I don't mean to seem blasé about it; my brushes with adversity have certainly not left me stronger right away. I don't think that's how it works. There's the whole "what doesn't kill you makes you stronger" trope but I'm sure that doesn't always work, either. See above.

Karsten had so much curiosity about everything and everyone. He was a gifted conversationalist, always asking people provocative and relevant questions and listening attentively to their answers. He brought a bottle of bourbon to every party not because he was an instigator, although maybe he was a little of that, too, but more because he saw how people shook off their shells when they loosened up. He was wry, witty, observant, and fun.

I can't compare our brains and how they work because we weren't wired the same. It isn't a fair or flattering comparison for either of us. And I would never want to be glib about that. But my priority now must be to understand how adversity affects me, and not dwell on how it affected him.

So I'm curious when I consider my own reaction to hard times, and why it is that I so often seem to see difficult situations for the opportunities they present and not as much for the disappointments they present. Why I see moments of joy and meaningfulness even in the midst of anguish. I *think* I've cultivated it, but I'd be lying if I claimed to be sure.

In any case, what has resonated with me most about grief since Karsten died is the idea of forward motion. Actually, I find it resonant even in less life-altering circumstances. I missed a flight a few years ago and was frustrated of course, but immediately began trying to make progress on getting to my destination and that became my focus, rather than my feelings of frustration. And once the problem is solved and I'm on the plane, those feelings of frustration are moot or diminished anyway.

"Getting to my destination" was a bit of a heavy-handed metaphor back there, I know. We all know the notion that life is about the journey. It's about progress, and how we move through it.

Admittedly, it's a pretty big claim to suggest that that's how I responded to Karsten's death. And yet, at some level, it was. Because I was the one who found him, the initial feelings of shock and horror were rapidly displaced by the realization that I needed to call 911, and by helping guide the first responders where they needed to go, and so on. Only once I was surrounded by friends who were taking care of everything for me did I really feel that I had nothing I could or should do, and still I repeatedly said "I just wish I knew what I was supposed to be *doing.*" That's my bias for action and motion. My friends wisely said that sitting on the couch just as I was was what I was supposed to be doing. And I did. And I processed. That was the action that was needed at that moment. And that moved me forward.

On Choosing What to Keep

Nashville, TN
July 22, 2012.

Tomorrow it will have been four weeks since Karsten died. Wednesday will be one month.

Dates have been whizzing by me while I try to get back to my life, to the extent that that's been possible, and I find here and there I've lost track of how many days or weeks it's been. Not that it really matters anyway: every seemingly insignificant moment has the potential to bring about some subtle new realization in how to heal. There's no calendar for that kind of thing.

It's like trying to decide when our relationship began. We kissed on the night we first met - did it begin then? We always celebrated that date as our "meeting anniversary" so sure, in one respect it was the beginning. But a few days passed before our next date (which was, of course, our first date) where sitting across from each other at dinner felt like floating in some warm ocean of both excitement and calm and you're dizzy and happy and you never want to get out. And then a day or two later, we spent our first night together and it was amazing and then maybe a few weeks later, we moved in together... you get the idea. Love unfolds in layers, even when it happens lightning fast.

> "Why is it we don't always recognize the moment when love begins, but we always know when it ends?"
>
> - Steve Martin (as Harris K. Telemacher) in "L.A. Story" (1991)

The finality of that quote probably makes me sound more morose than I am. The truth – the astonishing truth – is that I'm OK. Or at least I'm on the road to OK, and I have a full enough tank to get there, and I'll probably arrive before anyone expects. I didn't predict that. I always thought that if Karsten died, I wouldn't be able to survive the loss. I mean it: I truly, honestly didn't think I would go on breathing. But the weird and maybe ultimately logical thing is that the simple act of surviving something as catastrophic as finding your beloved partner dead – well, it feels very much like a "kill you or make you stronger" moment, and it didn't actually kill me. So as it turns out, I guess I've gotten stronger.

Of course – of course - there's a sizable part of me that wishes I could still be with him, but I can also see the years we spent together as a gift, rather than seeing the years we lost as a theft.

I'm totally broken about it in some ways, and looking at photos and watching the few videos I have of him are simultaneously comforting and painful, but what isn't broken is my ability to love: I know I'll love Karsten for the rest of my life; I love the friends who have stepped up to surround me with caring and generosity and safety and support; and at some point in the not-too-distant future, I will, almost certainly, begin to love someone else, because above all that's the message in this that resounds for me: life is too short and too fragile to miss any moment when you could be loving someone.

When my dad died in 2005, I read the poem "In Blackwater Woods" at his funeral, and the last part of it has been echoing back through my head since Karsten died:

To live in this world

you must be able

to do three things:

to love what is mortal;

to hold it

against your bones knowing

your own life depends on it;

and, when the time comes to let it go,

to let it go.

It's not as easy a process as the poem suggests, that whole "let it go" thing. But I'm figuring it out, day by day, hour by hour. The trick, I realized, is choosing what you'll let yourself keep. I already own, deep down, a lot of wonderful, meaningful, life-changing things about Karsten and this love we shared for nearly fifteen years. And they're aspects of him and his impact on me that I'll want to hold onto forever. The rest of this I can let slowly fall away.

And by doing that, I get a clearer glimpse of my life ahead of me having definition beyond tragedy: when the number of people I haven't seen since Karsten died will decrease, and every interaction won't begin or end with condolences or questions. I'm already stronger than some might suspect, and I keep getting stronger. And there's this: I know I have love still to give. I'm good at it. When a relationship lasts and works, it's not only because you fell in love however many years ago; it's because you give each other enough room to be yourselves, and because each of you adapts and learns to love each other for the people you grow into, day after day, time and time again. I've been genuinely, beautifully in love with the same person for well over a third of my life, but it's because I fell in love so many times with the ever-evolving version of who he really was, as he did for me. A part of me, a big part of me, will always love him. But I want the rest of my life to be the total package, too: the highs that inevitably bring the lows, not a compromised lesser version based in the fear of the possibility that I might lose love again. I could never trade amazing for adequate.

So it comes back to holding onto only what matters, what won't weigh you down, what strengthens you, and what prepares you for the rest of your life, rather than what anchors you to the past and kills you even while you're alive. It comes back to what you choose to keep.

As for me, I choose beauty. I choose to engage with people and to try, if I can, to create a moment of art out of conversation. I choose to see life and the world and everything in it as clearly as I can see it, and to honor the truth about it, even if it's harsh. I choose good times and happiness and laughter, as often as I can. And no matter what the potential is for loss, I will always, always choose love.

CHAPTER FOUR

OVERWHELM AND LEANING

Precognition

Nashville, TN
2013.

At some level I think maybe I always knew, with Karsten, that he'd be gone suddenly.

In the last few years especially, I used to pull my car up to the curb as I got home from work and maybe two or three days out of five I'd suddenly feel a strong anxiety that I was about to walk in and find him dead. He would often ride his bike at night from our house in the Historic Germantown neighborhood of Nashville the mile and a half or so to Lower Broadway so that he could wander amid the drunken tourists, and I often worried that I would get a phone call informing me that he'd been hit by a car in the low-lit streets between downtown and our neighborhood, or that he'd been stabbed or shot at a honky-tonk at two in the morning simply because he was in the wrong place at the wrong time when some whiskey-and-testosterone-fueled fist-fight turned tragically violent.

Perhaps this was all due to an overactive imagination, and perhaps I had a protective instinct hardwired into my mind that worked overtime because I loved him so much. But I also felt — no, I felt that I *knew* — that losing him would kill me. I feared he would die, and I believed I wouldn't survive his death. I would simply cease to breathe, or my heart would stop, because the idea of living without him was too absurd to ever be possible.

When I woke up that Monday morning and he wasn't in bed, that dread began to stir, even though it wasn't terribly unusual for him not to be in bed when I woke up. His pattern was to see me off to sleep around 10 PM, and then either to head down into his basement studio to work on an art project or into the home office at the back of the house to watch a movie on his computer, or to take a swig of bourbon before heading out on his bike toward downtown to watch the tourists get drunk on Broadway. And in the latter case, he often came home drenched in second-hand smoke, so on those nights he would set out a makeshift bed made of floor pillows and a comforter in the home office so as not to contaminate our bed with the smell of smoke. Or sometimes he'd fold out the sofa bed in the living room if he felt like he was going to have trouble sleeping and didn't want to wake me. (I'm a light sleeper.) So when I got up out of bed around 6 AM, tucking my bathrobe around me, I peeked around the corner into the home office. But there were no floor pillows set out, and no Karsten. I padded out through the kitchen to the living room, but he wasn't on the sofa bed. I looked in the front hallway and didn't see his bike, which he usually left out overnight because putting it away when he returned from his late night ride might wake me. (A really light sleeper.) When I saw that his bike wasn't there, the thought occurred to me that he'd been hit. And with that thought, I was instantly in the familiar zone of chilling dread.

My adrenaline was surging as I walked back to the back of the house again to look once more in the home office. This time I noticed a piece of paper lying in the middle on the floor. It was a full-page, full-color print-out of a picture of Karsten's car parked in the back yard, and in the bottom margin, he'd written, in his typical neat all-caps lettering, "CALL PARAMEDICS".

I pulled open the blinds to look into the back yard and there indeed was his car. I was surprised to see no apparent dent in the front — because the note made me assume an accident. I don't know what I thought the logistics of that were, given the note, but it was the first disconnected conclusion I had reached. But then my senses started to click together and I realized that I was looking at someone actually in the car, presumably Karsten, and that presumably he was injured. I moved immediately toward the back door to go to him and somehow had the presence of mind to stop and go back to the kitchen to the alarm control panel to disarm it before hurrying to the back door and outside to the car. As I approached, my view through the car windows became more clear and I could see that he was sideways in the back seat, hanging. I heard myself chanting a shaky "No, no, no, no" over and over as I got to the driver's side back door and opened it. I could see that he was immobile in a way that I knew, even with my limited exposure to death up-close, must have meant it was over. Still, I lifted his hair to see what I could of his face and saw a blueish tinge in his skin. I processed it instantly. He was gone. My life had entirely, materially, fundamentally changed.

I had stuck my cell phone in my bathrobe pocket as a matter of habit when I left the bedroom, so I took a deep breath and pulled it out and made my first-ever 911 call. It was important to me, for some reason, to remain calm and professional as I explained the situation to the operator. The entire back yard scene had given me the surreal sense of being trapped in a movie, but telling the operator that my husband had hanged himself in the car in our back yard took the surreal feeling to such a heightened level that I almost felt I was lying. Almost. She asked that I try to cut him down, and I tried to explain that I was unable. (I had a severe back injury that had caused a loss of grip and strength in my hands and arms, and at the time I barely had the strength to cut an apple, let alone saw through a makeshift noose made from a woven fabric belt.) We went back and forth about whether I should, or could, cut him down for what felt like a bizarre and dizzying amount of time, before eventually she told me that the police had arrived, which was an even more bizarre thing to hear as I stood still alone in the morning quiet of my back yard. I realized they must be at the front door, so my first-ever 911 call ended and I headed back into the house to meet the police.

I tried to invite the officers to come through the house, but they said they'd go around the side of the house, so I rushed back through the house to meet them outside as they did so. When I returned to the back yard, less than three minutes after I'd left it, it seemed to me to be filled with police and paramedics. One officer approached me as I emerged from the back door of the house and asked me "do you know this man?"

"Yes," I said indignantly. "That's my husband."

The officer from the front door had come up the steep side walkway and just caught up to me, and having witnessed that exchange, he clearly sized up the potential for pointless distress and said "alright, let's go inside" and led me back into the house he'd just avoided walking through.

When we got to the kitchen, he asked me if I had anyone I could call. I thought of my close friend Jen and tapped her name in my phone's favorites list, but I heard it ring once and immediately hung up with the thought that maybe it was too early to call. I then thought of my neighbor Paige who is often out walking at that time of the morning, so I called her and asked her to come over without explaining why. She didn't ask. The officer met her at the front door and explained what happened. Jen called me back, having seen the missed phone call, and Paige explained what happened. Jen and her husband came over right away. Jen started calling my family and friends, and explaining what happened. That whole morning, I never explained to anyone what happened.

Paige went home and came back with a strong pot of coffee and a light blue mug. (I still have the mug. I've tried to return it a few times; she has gently insisted I hang on to it.)

I sat shakily on the sofa and sipped coffee as the police filed their reports and asked a few questions, and my friends made phone calls, and more friends arrived with grocery bags filled with food, and still more friends arrived and watered the yard and swept the front steps and cleaned the cat litter boxes, and the morning turned into day.

So Long, 2012, You Axe-Wielding Psycho
* * *

Nashville, TN
    December 31, 2012.

I'll tell you straight up: 2012 seemed as if it came at me like a psycho with an axe.

I mean, intense personal loss is usually enough to color the character of an entire calendar year. Going through a nearly year-long period of physical pain would probably be sufficient grounds to write the year off as frustrating at best. But between Karsten's death in June and the near-disability that resulted from multiple bulging discs from May through December, my entire life was thrown into chaos. My ability to focus was strained considerably, to say the least. I had planned early on for a big year for my company, gearing up new programs and growing sales and staff, and we did do well — really well, all things considered — but that growth was scaled back drastically from what I anticipated and hoped for. To complicate things further, in addition to my own challenges, literally dozens of my friends went through divorces and breakups and other personal losses, and the impact on my social circles and the community overall was seismic. At this point, you can probably picture 2012, the axe-wielding psycho, in position and ready to chop.

But in the midst of all that insanity, the year did a few things right, if you tilt your head at a certain angle. It taught me how to ask for (and accept) help. It showed me how loving and supportive my friends, family, staff, and community are. And it showed me how strong and resilient I always hoped I was, but never had proof of. Now I do.

Because it would have been damned easy to assume a victim mentality this year, and I resisted indulging in it. It would have been easy beyond description to dwell in depression, despair, or at least a deep melancholy, and truthfully some of that was, at a few points, unavoidable and, I do realize, perfectly reasonable. But even throughout those times, I adamantly sought joyful moments and meaningful interactions, and so much more often than not, I found them.

So even if 2012 wasn't an axe-wielding psycho, as it is totally tempting to claim, it was at least something of a scenery-chewing bad actor that didn't know when enough was enough. Yet, as Karsten always said, you have more to learn from a bad example than a good one. And as much as I'd like to give 2012 the middle finger as it ham-handedly exits the stage, I think instead I'll give it credit for demonstrating some toughlove lessons, and leave it at that.

One of the biggest of those lessons has been that when life knocks you on your ass, there's nothing so motivating as the simple triumph of getting up and moving forward. And even when moving forward isn't possible, merely looking forward will do.

So in the spirit of looking and moving forward, I'm batting my eyelashes at 2013 and smiling my best smile. What I'm hoping for is this:

- to remember how to ask for and accept help, and become more resourceful and self-reliant anyway
- to maintain the strength of the friendships that formed in the midst of crisis and chaos this summer and beyond
- to keep enjoying life's pleasures, however small, however fleeting, even when the odds seemed stacked in favor of sadness.

A year from now, when I write a reflection on 2013, I hope I can sigh with delight and say it was my best year yet. And I hope you will, too. But in case it turns out to be psychotic, stick with me. I already know how to get through a crazy year.

Grace or Casseroles? A Non-Believer's Musings on Prayer

Nashville, TN
   March 23, 2008.

I was reading Elizabeth Gilbert's "Eat, Pray, Love" on one of my flights a few weeks ago. (It's a wonderfully insightful and beautifully written book; I highly recommend it.) There's a passage where the author, having recently developed a personal relationship with prayer and a self-styled spirituality, is describing an exchange with her pragmatic sister, Catherine.

> A family in my sister's neighborhood was recently stricken with a double tragedy when both the mother and her three-year-old son were diagnosed with cancer. When Catherine told me about this, I could only say, shocked, "Dear God, that family needs grace." She replied firmly, "That family needs casseroles," and then proceeded to organize the entire neighborhood into bringing the family dinner, in shifts, every single night, for an entire year. I do not know if my sister fully recognizes that this is grace.

Karsten and I got talking about my father's death. My father was a popular man, loved by many in his town and with a wide circle of friends and family across the country. Many people were praying for him as he waged his fight with cancer. Some people would probably conclude that the prayers must not have been very effective since the cancer ultimately won. But even as a non-spiritual person, I think that's an unfair characterization of the effects of that praying. I would never attempt to claim that there is no power in prayer. I just don't think it's the only vehicle for the conveyance of caring, and it's loaded with religious affiliation, which has no appeal to me. But I have no trouble accepting the possibility, perhaps not as a direct result of prayer, but perhaps resulting indirectly from the quantities of people who simply told my father and the rest of his family that they were praying for him, that my father died with more awareness of how loved he was, and that we, his family, could accept his death with more comfort because we knew how loved he was.

Maybe you wouldn't call that the power of prayer, per se. And I would agree that it's something different, but I think — and this is a non-believer attempting to understand the minds of believers, so I may have it entirely wrong — but I think there's something uniquely potent about prayer to a believer that is somehow not present in the offerings of "thoughts" or "good vibes" or "positive energy," or any number of alternatives I or anyone else might suggest.

That's the struggle I have as a non-believer who wants to offer comfort to my loved ones. I wish I had something I could offer my cousin's family as they're dealing with my 17-year-old cousin battling lymphoma. I have told them I'm thinking about them, but I feel acutely that that's not as powerful a statement as telling someone you're praying for them. To my eyes, as a non-believer, that's the power of prayer: a communication shortcut that says you want to intercede for someone; that you feel their situation merits grace, and you're looking to powers bigger than yourself to provide it.

But without that communication shortcut, I guess I find myself in the role of the pragmatic sister, trying to think of when and how to make the proverbial (or literal) casseroles and hope that they are received as grace. (Here I should mention how humbling it is to have a sister who is both a praying person and a casserole maker in the most active sense — she was recently awarded Citizen of the Year in her hometown for her efforts in setting up a non-profit organization that helps the poor and needy in her otherwise well-to-do suburb. She's a double-helping of grace.) What I lack in spiritual connection with believers perhaps I make up for in compassion, but how can I be of much practical use to a family hundreds of miles away? There's a missing ingredient that could help bridge the distance, and to say "I'm thinking of you" sounds hollow.

I suppose it's relevant in some way that I'm musing about this on Easter morning. I have no real ties to Easter: nothing about its religious implications carries weight with me, and the childhood chocolate-fest is behind me. Even the pagan traditions offer little to the pragmatic, so it's simply a Sunday when more businesses are shuttered than usual. But there is something attractive about the hope of renewal, the rituals of rebirth that carry through from the pagan to the Christian traditions, in welcoming spring and recognizing the cyclical nature of life. (Maybe it's the gardener in me.) I know I'm looking for a chance to discover something in myself — some offering I can provide to those who need comfort that feels as powerful as prayer and does as much good as casseroles.

I don't expect to find the answer today. But I'm asking the question, and questions are more important than answers.

CHAPTER FIVE
DEALING WITH FINALITY

Drawing to a Close

Park Forest, IL
   October 18, 2005.

My dad is dying, but typical of my dad, he's being stubborn about it. If the doctors say he has days, maybe a week, then by god, a week comes and goes and he's smiling and having a rare good day at the end of that week. If we get the impression, as we have several times, that this day might be his last, then by god, the next day he's alert and nearly talkative, and we're left scratching our heads and drying our tears and just trying to ride out the emotional tidal waves.

My mom and I went to meet with the people at the funeral home a few weeks ago. Fortunately, my dad already made all his arrangements six years ago when his cancer was first diagnosed as malignant. Unfortunately, the funeral home guys fell somewhere between sleazy used car salesman stereotype and good cop / bad cop / Keystone Cops, and although I found it all absurdly funny, I don't know that my mom was as ready to see the humor in the ordeal.

If there's one bright spot in this sea of surreal darkness, it's that my sister and I have largely reconciled. It's a long story, but it comes down to what my coworker and friend Keith described as sounding "like a Lifetime original movie." A significant letter that apparently never arrived at its destination, a conversation where both participants had completely different understandings of what was said, that sort of thing. And that's the basis of what's been keeping us distant for lo these last nine years. So while things aren't perfect now, there are signs that our relationship may improve with time. And I think my dad has been coherent enough to realize that, which must help him feel a little more at ease, since I know the strained relations between my sister and me have bothered him terribly.

For a long time, I was worried my brother didn't get the whole thing — he has learning and developmental disabilities — but several people within and outside of the family have made efforts to make sure he understands. Now he's acting out in ways that suggest he gets it and isn't ready to handle it very well. Which, let's be honest, is how the rest of us pretty much feel, too.

And my mom is struggling hardest of all. Her husband of 40 years, her closest and dearest friend by far, and clearly the best companion the universe could have ever invented for her, is becoming — or perhaps has already become — unrecognizable to her, and she's still feeding him, bathing him, and performing plenty of other thankless tasks out of love and duty and determination to see him die with whatever dignity is still possible at this point. Her dilemma breaks my heart every day, and as stressed out and wound-up as she definitely is, she bears it all so much better than I can ever imagine doing myself.

And Karsten — well, what can I possibly say about Karsten that does him justice? After losing his mother seven months ago, I'm sure it's suffocating for him to be in an environment where the reality of parental death is thick in the air. But he knows I need him with me, and he's there for me. We're in this together, after all, and thank the universe or whatever divine there may or may not be for that. This man is like oxygen to me — I simply can't imagine breathing without him. Especially not right now. And he's consistently the one person who can relax me, who can always make me laugh (even when it's a dark laugh shared in a silent glance across the room), with whom I can just walk and walk and walk for hours and talk about anything or talk about nothing — and it's the only kind of therapy that could possibly do me any good right now.

He soothes my soul.

So there it is, in a nutshell. The cast of characters, the somber scene, the barely-crawling pace of it all. It's draining as hell, and I feel like I'm in limbo no matter where I am, but I'm trying to make the best of it and find the moments of levity, the revelations of truth, the opportunities to draw closer with the people from whom I've moved away so many times — and trying to laugh and love as much as possible at all times. I think that's all there is to do. I guess that's all there is for any of us to do.

My Beautiful, Unreliable Memory

Nashville, TN
February 15, 2015.

I've been thinking a lot about memory today. My cat Barbra Streisand died yesterday. He (yes, he) was 18 years old and spent about 16 of those years with me, until he developed some kind of cancer that reared up suddenly and took him down hard. I was looking through old pictures of him yesterday and today, and each one called to mind such a vivid moment — Barbra with a funny face while playing, Barbra with a comically menacing posture while fighting with his brother, Barbra adorably poking his head out from under a sheet — that my mind could somehow almost animate around the snapshot, but I couldn't always stitch the snapshots together. And I couldn't necessarily remember much that might have happened in between the time of the snapshots.

And what I could remember I wasn't sure about. Like Bonnie's death. Four years ago, almost to the day, Barbra's sister Bonnie had to be put down. She'd been diagnosed with a squamous cell carcinoma on her tongue nearly a year prior, and had undergone a procedure to remove as much of the growth from her tongue as possible without making life difficult for her, and we'd been giving her medication to slow the growth of the tumor for months. But one morning I almost couldn't tell if she was alive or dead until I got close to her, and it was obvious the other shoe had dropped, and thankfully Karsten, my late husband, and I came to the same conclusion at once: that Bonnie was gone enough that it was only a short matter of time before she'd starve on her own, and that making the decision to end her life perhaps a day or a few days earlier than it otherwise would would be the kindest thing, even if it was difficult for us. But no, the thing was, the decision was surprisingly not difficult. After knowing for months that we'd probably have to come to that moment, the moment itself was surprisingly clear.

That wasn't the case with Barbra. He'd been slowly showing signs of age for a few years, developing arthritis and having some difficulty with some of the jumps he used to make to get up and down from high shelves where he and the other cats sleep away the day. But he'd been mostly alright until this past Thursday night when I went to feed the cats, and he didn't move from where he'd been lying. And he didn't eat when I set out the food. And he struggled to drink. And so on.

The next day, the vet said "tumor" and it all came back. The struggle to give Bonnie a good quality of life for the last months. The ultimate decision. I even flashed back to watching my dad die slowly from cancer ten years ago. I'd had months to accept the outcome with my dad, and with Bonnie, too. I had to process it all in a day with Barbra. Rationally I knew he wasn't going to be getting any better. He was four years older than Bonnie'd been when she died. At 14, death for Bonnie felt a little premature. At 18, death for Barbra seemed imminent.

But all of that is to say that the main thing I was remembering about Bonnie's death is: I don't remember it. I mean, I do, but I don't. I can't recall now the exact context of the conversation, but a few years ago I remember saying to Karsten that if for some reason I'd had to go by myself to take her in to be euthanized, I wasn't sure I could have managed to do it. Because somehow I'd come to remember him taking her in by himself. He looked at me quizzically and said "What do you mean? You did everything when Bonnie died. You called the vet, you drove, you carried her in to the office, you held her and petted her throughout the injection. I was there but I was a wreck." That's not at all how I had it in my mind, but he sounded so sure and described it so clearly, so my imagination tried out that image. Something about it seemed familiar. And maybe I felt just a little bit proud of having been

43

strong enough to do what he said I did, so I guess I accepted that version as true once I heard it.

But maybe that's all memory really is: the version of the story that seems to suit us best.

When I think back to what I first remember about Barbra, it starts with a story about Karsten.

Karsten begged for cats. Well, that's the way we always liked to tell the story. I don't know that he begged.

Karsten had not grown up an animal lover. He'd not even much liked them until sometime in his 30s when he got high in the home of a friend who had a cat. Observing this cat while stoned somehow allowed him to appreciate the intricacies of the quirky feline mystique, and he was hooked. (On the cat, not on the drug.) But scraping by as a working artist in the Bay Area in low-income rental apartments had not allowed him the luxury to take in an animal friend.

After we met and started dating, we pretty quickly established that neither of us wanted kids. I thought maybe I wanted a dog. I always considered myself a dog person, and imagined adopting a lovable mutt who'd accompany me on road trips and be my constant companion. He wanted a cat, or maybe two cats. He begged (maybe). I agreed.

For months before we adopted any cats, Karsten and I had been visiting shelters on weekend afternoons, spending time meeting dozens, maybe hundreds, of different cats and getting to know their personalities so we would recognize the traits that suited us best. We couldn't adopt any yet because our apartment wouldn't allow it, but we'd found a place to move in together after a few months that would. We moved into our new apartment on December 1st, 1998. On December 2nd, we drove from San Jose to the San Francisco SPCA, accompanied by our friend Jean who loved cats and shared in our excitement. The day we adopted Barbra and the Littermates (that was the name of their band, we liked to say), we had browsed through the entire place and not been particularly enamored with any of the cats we met until we got to the very last hallway (the way the story goes) and I noticed two of these cats peeking out the door at the very end of the hallway. (It was me who first noticed them in my memory of it. I wonder if that's true.)

I think what happened is that we adopted cats and loved them and became cat people, and I got hooked. I always went with the story that Karsten begged for cats, and he did start the whole thing, but after we'd adopted the first three, the next three were probably more my idea. I've played into the reluctant cat person narrative, but I think my enthusiasm is more the truth.

Barbra was always a great cat. I am confident in that memory. Nothing clouds it. He was sociable and always interested in meeting new people. He was hilariously gluttonous, as he demonstrated when we tried to introduce unlimited food dispensers to lower the maintenance while we traveled. He stood in front of it eating and eating and eating, then sat down and continued to eat, then actually lay down on his side with his neck craned over the edge of the dish so that he could still eat. He and Baby Clyde gained 50% of their body weight in a few months thanks to that feeder, so we had to go back to portion control. He was adventurous and tough. He was the only cat I ever walked on a leash around the neighborhood, because he was up for it and cooperative enough to make it work. He was easygoing and affectionate, but he stood his ground if another cat challenged him.

After Karsten died two and a half years ago, I spent a lot of time on the living room sofa, just sitting. Just trying to let it sink in. Barbra spent a lot of time with me. Baby Clyde did, too. I don't know what they processed about Karsten's absence, but I know they knew something was wrong because there were so many people in the house and yet I wasn't moving from my spot on the sofa. So they just sat with me.

Ten years ago, when we moved into the house where we now live, Karsten and I introduced the cats to the house in the bedroom we intended as their home base of sorts. We let them out of their carriers to explore and sniff, and the other cats went off to explore every corner and shelf of the room. Except for Barbra. He gave a few tentative sniffs, then hopped up on the futon where we sat to be with me and Karsten. He seemed to be saying he'd be alright. He'd adjust. He just wanted to hang out with us a while.

At least that's how I remember it.

When At Last You Reach the End, Turn Around and Start Again

Park Forest, IL
November 5, 2005.

When your cell phone rings at 2:35 AM, you can be sure it's a call you wish you didn't have to take.

I marveled at how calm my mother managed to sound as she said, "Your father passed."

I took some time to completely fall apart in the hotel room, with Karsten comforting me. It's amazing how a hurt that has ached so much for so long is still able to hurt so much more.

After a bit, I dressed and drove over to my parents' house, where my sister, my brother and his wife, and the hospice nurse all were. They were all in the bedroom with his body when I arrived, so I hesitantly went in. You know, it's true what they say about how you can tell when life has left the body – it just lies there looking so empty, dull, and useless after the life is gone.

When the hospice nurse asked about whether we wanted him buried with his wedding ring (incidentally, no, my mom wants to keep it) and any other personal effects, my sister mentioned that the Livestrong bracelet he's been wearing without removing for years now should stay with him. A few months ago, my Livestrong bracelet broke and I hadn't wanted to replace it because I wanted to forget about cancer and death whenever I could. But at that moment, I knew that wearing his bracelet would mean so much more to me. My mom loved the idea, and my sister was initially hesitant until she thought of putting a new one on him before the wake.

So she and I carefully took it from his wrist, and I'm wearing it now. She's bringing a new one for him later today.

By 5:30 AM, the funeral directors had arrived to take Dad's body away, and we'd spent enough time with it to feel ready to let it go. He wasn't there anymore, anyway — the best of him has been leaving us for months, and the last of him had been gone for hours.

My sister went home to talk to her kids. My brother and his wife went home. I made the first calls to a designated contact on each side of the family. The hospice nurse finished her paperwork, disposed of Dad's medications, and left. And my mom and I went to see if we could manage to eat some breakfast.

Everyone knows the cliche about how you always hear the worst possible music at a time like this, right? Can you guess? How about Rod Stewart's cover of "They Can't Take That Away From Me" playing in the restaurant while we're struggling to eat? We were crying as quietly and discreetly as we could, and I pointed out how much I hate Rod Stewart, which made my mom laugh.

Anyway, that's about the latest. I'll post more later, I'm sure.

The Happiness List

Nashville, TN
June 2012.

I had barely moved from the center of the sofa in the living room in the two days since Karsten had died. It was where the police officer who first responded to my 911 call had led me to sit down that first morning, and it was near the front door, where close friends were beginning to arrive and congregate, and so I just stayed there in my robe and slippers, which is what I was wearing when I'd found him. Eventually, as people arrived to bring food and show support, I found the wherewithal to slip away to our bedroom — make that *my* bedroom — and put on loose-fitting yoga pants and a tee-shirt. That first night, I'd slept in our bed — *my* bed — and when I got up, I put on the same loose pants and tee-shirt and made my way back to the sofa. I recall someone, maybe my mother, asking me if I wanted to shower, but I said no. I can't remember if that was on the first day or the second. I wasn't collapsed in a heap in the corner, but sitting in the center of the sofa was feeling like the best I could reasonably do.

But sometime on the third day, after reluctantly deciding that I owed it to the dozens of people who were dropping by to have a shower and put on a new pair of loose yoga pants and a fresh tee-shirt, I had just settled back into my place on the sofa when I had a sudden realization that it was Wednesday. I sprang up and nearly sprinted to the back of the house.

Because the recycling truck comes on Tuesdays, but not every Tuesday. Every third Tuesday, but not always then either. If this was the one time when the truck had come on schedule, if yesterday had even been the schedule, and if one of the many friends wandering the house looking for ways to help had been organized enough to think to take out the recycling from the home office, then his papers might already be gone.

Karsten always carried a pad of paper and a pen. The night I met him at a party fifteen years before, when I went to give him my phone number, he whipped out the pen and pad, and the nearby partygoers all teased him that he was a player.

The paper recycling bin in the home office was full, to my relief. I dumped the bin on the floor, and sifted through each piece of paper. Mixed in with envelopes from bills and letters were crumpled bits of paper, some crumpled so tightly into balls that I had to use the tips of my fingernails to loosen them. I had to work to control the shaking of my body and my breathless sobbing to keep from destroying the papers, but the more I tried to undo the wads of paper, the clearer my understanding became of how tightly he must have been clenching the balls of paper to make them so compact, and through the paper I could feel his utter anguish and despair.

Eventually I recovered a stack of papers that filled an accordion file.

Among those papers were many idea sketches for future art projects, and a small slip on which he'd been writing his Happiness List. Making the Happiness List was something a book he'd been reading suggested doing. He'd been struggling with his creative vision, and when he struggled with his creative vision he also struggled with depression. This was not new; this was the pattern of our lives over many years. But over those years I'd seen him experience unexpected happiness time and time again by doing things he loved, and I agreed with the book that it might do him some good to take some inventory of that.

He'd made an effort to make the list, but it wasn't very long, and the ideas were mostly a recap of some fun things he'd done or we'd both done recently. The list wasn't nearly as long or diverse as I knew the real list of things that gave him some happiness to be. Maybe he couldn't imagine himself happy through the fog of depression. Maybe happiness seemed not only unreachable from there but even an incomprehensible idea, alien and strange and very removed from the floor where he sat with his pen and notepad.

Looking through those papers was an aching reminder to me of his despair. And it made me feel sure that I'd misunderstood the breadth and depth of his depression, in a way that even the fact of his suicide hadn't made as clear. And it began to sink in that I might have known, sort of, but I probably couldn't have known, really. As much as we understood each other, as much as I knew his tastes and his preferences and his humor and his love and his touch and his tendencies and so much more about him, I didn't know this aspect of his reality.

After that it didn't ache any less and I didn't understand it all any better, but it started to make me feel like maybe not understanding it was going to be a way of understanding it. And that somehow something about that felt like a kind of understanding. And as much as this reality hurt to process, I had to admit that I felt like I had come to understand Karsten a little better.

The Kind You're Not Prepared For

49

* * *

Miami, FL
  March 2005.

Every few weeks my work sent me on various trips around the country, mostly to fairly unglamorous destinations, with not much in common with a vacation. Karsten was focused on our songwriting and his visual art, so a good deal of his work was portable, which meant he could often accompany me, spending the days working in the hotel room or exploring the surroundings on foot while I went off to meetings, conferences, speaking engagements, you name it. And in the evenings when I was free, we could regroup and explore the area some more together. It was fun even in the small towns. It was especially fun whenever I hit jackpot with a trip like Miami.

On that particular trip, we booked ourselves into a hotel on the beach, and every day I'd go to my meetings while he wrote or strolled up and down the shore. The first evening, our plan was to meet back up for dinner with one of my colleagues. I got back to the room a little early and we were just about to take off walking down the beach when his phone rang — it was his sister. She was upset: their mom was in the hospital. The details were fuzzy at first. Should we go to be with them? No, we were told; stay put and they'll keep us updated.

His parents had just driven through Nashville and visited with us days before on their way back to their home in northern Indiana from their favorite spot in Florida. We'd all been amused by the coincidence of the timing and joked that they were handing off the responsibilities of keeping Florida warm. But the long drive must have been a strain, as it can be for anyone in even peak physical condition. I have to think that her restricted circulation from the long road trip damaged her body. But I don't know.

The next two days were an anxious quiet. I went to a few of my meetings, but bowed out of some of the activities where I wouldn't be missed to check back in on Karsten. During one of these trips back to the hotel room, he got the call. I could hear his sister crying from the other side of the bed where I was sitting. I could tell she wasn't actually able to speak, but we both knew his mother had died.

After he got that news, we sat in silence for a long time. I don't know what he was thinking, exactly, but I know I was thinking about how much it had always been clear that he loved his mother, how his complicated relationship with his father might be more complicated now, or perhaps easier in some way, how I knew his sister and mother were incredibly close and how devastated she must be, how close he and his sister were and how devastated he must be for her. I also thought about how my dad was starting to lose his battle with cancer, and how startling it was that this would happen first.

I offered to leave, suggested we both go to be with the family, or even that he go and I catch up, but he said there were no arrangements being made yet so he preferred to stay and be in a place with natural beauty to process it all.

The afternoon and evening were a sad quiet interrupted now and then by me asking a question — "Are you sure you don't want to go?" — and him answering. And then a return to quiet. Until we eventually got tired, and lay down to sleep on top of the bedspread, still dressed in the day's clothes.

The morning after, I slipped out for a run and tried to find comfort in the feeling of running. I tried to confront the grief, to pound it out through my feet. When that didn't work, I tried to escape every feeling but the exhilaration of running. When that didn't work, I slowed to a stop, turned around, and walked slowly back to the hotel.

It's a Long Drive Back to Nashville...

Nashville, TN
November 11, 2005.

It's a long drive back to Nashville but we made it in one piece. Well, two pieces, I suppose, counting me and Karsten separately.

I'm completely exhausted. Glad to be home, but have already cried twice tonight. I'm going to try going back to work on Monday. Here's hoping I hold it together.

We scaled the wake back to one evening instead of two, thank the powers that be. One evening of non-stop condolences was tough enough to get through. And then Thursday was the funeral services at the church and cemetery, followed by the funeral luncheon and after-luncheon gathering at my sister's house. It was a long day to finish a long week. And then, of course, there's the eight-hour drive today.

The wake was tough. My dad looked unrecognizable. I suppose he's been looking stranger and stranger as he got closer to the end, but it was only once they tried to make him up to look normal that he looked so shockingly weird. Everyone seemed to feel that way, and I took to warning people when they arrived to brace themselves if they planned to approach the casket. A lot of people thanked me afterwards for the warning.

I made a slide show of photos and ran it on my laptop on the other end of the room from the casket so that people would have something positive to focus their visual attention, and a lot of people thanked me for that, too. I'm pleased that it helped other people, but just making it was cathartic for me, so I hardly needed to watch it.

Also, at the funeral service in the church yesterday, my sister and I both gave eulogies, and although we hadn't compared notes or anything, people commented that it was nice how our statements echoed each other. I said it's easy to be consistent when you're telling the truth.

In case anyone would like to read it, here's what I said in the eulogy:

It's tempting to say that 2005 has been a bad year. I spent most of this year anxious and anticipating my father's death. I did not, as it happened, anticipate my mother-in-law's death. And watching my father die slowly took up the summer months and into the fall. So yes, it's tempting to say this has been a bad year.

But you, I, my father, all of us — we don't live in years. We don't die in years. We live — lived — in moments. A series of moments. A collection of moments. And yes, we die in moments.

You see, during these past few months, the concept of time has become surreal to me. There was, for example, the first day we all thought would be my father's last: the hours spent in vigil, five to ten minutes passing in silence, 20 to 30 seconds between each breath my father took. But he fooled us, and lived for weeks after that. Time is unreliable in our lives. Only moments matter.

And so I learned from this ordeal to make the most of moments. When my father was alert and talkative, I tried to use those moments to find out what he still needed in his life, what unfinished business he felt he had. And in the hours and

increasingly days that passed in
unresponsiveness, I learned to find comfort in the
memory of past moments — a skill that I hope
will comfort me for the rest of my life.

Some people live to be 104 years old. You might
say they're rich in years. Yet it's no guarantee
that they're rich in moments. My father lived
relatively few years. Yet I believe, and I suspect
my mother, for one, would agree, that my father
was a man rich in moments.

My dad was not the last year of his life. He was
not the moment of his death. He was — and, for
me, he will always be — the sum total of his
laughter and love, the gifts he gave me and the
extraordinary generosity with which he gave
them, the lessons I learned from him, the corny
jokes he told, the many kisses and hugs we
shared, his accomplishments, his friendships, his
ability to love and give and accept and learn and
love some more.

For all of its difficulty, 2005 has given me some of

my life's most precious moments so far. And we, as a species, are blessed with memory. So I can step forward into the next moments of my life, holding close my memories of the good, the sweet, the beautiful moments this year and all the years before it, and comforted by the memory of the moments I shared with my father.

I'm often told that I resemble my father in many ways: our appearance, our love of music, our aptitude with languages, and so on -- but I will be lucky if at the end of my years, I can know that I resembled him in this respect: that I lived a life abundant in love and rich in moments.

I would like to conclude these thoughts in the words of Mary Oliver, who wrote so eloquently about the illusion of time and the loss of what we love in the poem "In Blackwater Woods."

> Look, the trees
> are turning
> their own bodies

into pillars

of light,
are giving off the rich
fragrance of cinnamon
and fulfillment,

the long tapers
of cattails
are bursting and floating away over
the blue shoulders

of the ponds,
and every pond,
no matter what its
name is, is

nameless now.
Every year
everything
I have ever learned

in my lifetime
leads back to this: the fires

and the black river of loss
whose other side

is salvation,
whose meaning
none of us will ever know.
To live in this world

you must be able
to do three things:
to love what is mortal;
to hold it

against your bones knowing
that your own life depends on it;
and, when the time comes to let it go,
to let it go.

CHAPTER SIX

REBUILDING AND TRYING IT OUT

Is There a Groove to Get Back Into?

Nashville, TN
November 2005.

When I returned to work a week after my dad's funeral, still emotionally bruised and heavy, the first thing one of my coworkers said to me was "Glad you're back. You have *no idea* what we've been going through here."

All during the early part of my dad's cancer treatments, I was taking a day or two off every other month or so to go up to Chicago whenever he'd have chemo or radiation. My bosses asked me every time: didn't I want to take longer and be with my family? And I said no, what I'd like is, since I can see this isn't likely to get better, to be able to save up that time I would have taken and go for a longer stretch when he's dying so I can try to be helpful to my mom then. I hoped they would remember that I was trading off that time.

But my dad died more slowly than I could possibly have imagined, and what I thought would be a few extra days off turned into a week here and there. My employer had a policy where colleagues could donate paid time off to each other for hardship situations, and when I sent an email to some work friends asking if they could spare any, the word got around and I ended up with enough PTO to cover an extended time away. My bosses agreed to let me go, and I said I'd at least try to check in on email and see if I could make progress on some things from Chicago or on the road.

And in the end I was out of the office almost every other week in the summer and most of August, September, and October. And half of November, after he died on the 5th and we buried him on the 10th. I was back at work on the 17th.

I know most companies' bereavement leave policies are nowhere near that generous. But those policies simply don't align with what it means to have a dying parent, or partner, or anyone you dearly love. People need time to be with their loved ones when they're dying. I wouldn't have wanted to not have had the chance to help my mom take care of my dad. I wouldn't have wanted to leave the day after the funeral, when there was still so much to do and so much for the family to process.

Maybe that means a person in that situation should quit her job. Maybe take a formal leave of absence if the policies allow for that. I thought I had an understanding of an informal sort of leave of absence with my bosses and my team, particularly with all the donated PTO. But people have short memories, and the realities of their immediate environments tend to win out moment to moment over empathy for someone else's situation. I don't fault my coworkers for that, exactly. Although the majority of my coworkers were sympathetic and patient, my immediate coworkers had clearly had enough of my time away. But it was hard to come back to a team of people who were frustrated with me about the time I'd taken to be with my dying father and my family, especially since I'd tried at least a little bit to keep up with my work remotely.

So, let's just say it wasn't easy to be back.

Still, work was distracting, and sometimes that helped. But other times, I just wanted to curl up into a ball in a corner and cry and miss my daddy. And my perspective had shifted; I couldn't see what we were doing as important. It was a tough adjustment.

Eventually one day not too long after I got back, I quit. It was the first step toward building a life that suited the slightly broken but considerably more aware and resilient self I was becoming.

Baby Steps

Nashville, TN
July 2012.

There is an expression: the year of firsts, that describes the idea that everything you do becomes a first time again: the first time you go back to your favorite restaurant without your partner, the first time you drive again, the first time you take out the trash by yourself, the first time you trek your way through an airport alone.

All of it, every last bit of it, was profoundly different after Karsten died. Even after the dust settled, so to speak, I wasn't sure what I was looking at.

My employees had been doing a great job running things in my absence that first week and I'd been doing some work from home when it was truly needed, but I wanted to try to get back into the rhythm of going to my office, even if it was only for a little bit at a time just to experience the strange mechanics of it. It happened that July 4th — Independence Day — was only a week and a half after Karsten died, so, knowing that no one was likely to be around, I chose that day to walk back into the office. A friend went with me, and she sat nearby and worked on a laptop while I mindlessly checked some email and sorted a few files. We left after an hour. It was a start.

I went back to the office every single day after that, including weekends, adding a little more time to my visits each time. I wasn't doing meaningful work; I was just trying to build up the stamina to actually *stay* there, like a marathoner training for those 26.2 miles. It took me two weeks to build back up to a nearly full-time schedule, but my head still wasn't in it for quite some time after that.

It's kind of like when I quit smoking. I started when I was a kid, like 11 or 12, and I was 24 when I finally quit, but it took me about a dozen tries to really quit. Each time I planned to quit, I'd stumble across some context that made me want a cigarette. The first time, it was the seven-minute walk from my apartment in Chicago's Little Italy to my office at the University of Illinois at Chicago. Just about the perfect length of time for a leisurely smoke. After I'd decided to quit and then made that walk the following Monday, it made me want a cigarette, and I caved right away. I realized I'd need a substitute or something to take my mind off of wanting a cigarette. So I eventually found one, I tried to quit again, only to hit another wall a few weeks later. And again, I found a substitute, tried to quit again, and on it went like that for a few years until I'd finally exhausted all the obstacles. I've now been a non-smoker since 1998, but I first started quitting in 1996.

Discovering the triggers of grief turned out to be pretty similar. I'd go to the grocery store, no problem, and pull up in front of my house before remembering that carrying the bags up the stairs to the house used to be something Karsten would gallantly insist on doing. "Beautiful hands shouldn't have to lift heavy things," he'd say, and I'd comically roll my eyes at the sexism but smile at the kindness.

Or when I tried to take out trash and recycling to the back yard, and the car was still there where he'd hanged himself. I had to walk past it, and I'd slow down every time, looking in, remembering. I knew I had to get rid of the car eventually, but I also thought maybe I should keep it there until I could walk past it without slowing down. One day a few months later, when I was in a hurry, that finally happened. I realized as I was walking back into the house that I'd passed by the car without paying attention. I sold it the following week.

Finding Your New Identity

Nashville, TN
March 31, 2014.

* * *

I remember having flashes of worry, early on, that when I made my way back out into the dating world, I was going to be undateable. It wasn't a self-esteem issue: I was thinking about my busy work life, my cats, even my online presence, and, of course, the baggage I would now carry as a widow.

And then almost at the same moments, I would think with guarded excitement about the possibility that there might still be great love out there for me to find and experience.

Which is why it was only seven weeks after Karsten died that I asked a friend to lunch and asked him to ask me to dinner. He was taken aback by the suggestion — it had to be too soon, right? — but I just adamantly wanted to feel forward motion and I wanted to laugh, and he was always good to hang out with for laughs. So with my reassurance that it was a good idea, he asked me out, and we dated discreetly for the next few months, but the timing of it really was a little too abrupt and the whole thing never felt quite right. It was a good transition, though, and I'm grateful for it and for him.

When it had become clear that it was time to move on, online dating seemed like the logical next step. It turned out to be a fantastic idea: the simple act of filling out an online dating profile forced me to confront the reality of who I was without Karsten in a very intentional way. Describing myself, my interests, and my tastes turned into a major act of healing. I didn't want to surgically remove Karsten's influence from my answers, but I didn't want to leave it there without asking whether I had my own preference independent of his.

When you've been tightly partnered with someone for nearly fifteen years, even when each of you has your own strong personality, there is a dissolving and merging of identity that takes place. That movie we watched 10 times — was it him who liked that movie so much or did I? Did we eat at that restaurant so often because we enjoyed it so much or because it was habit and we enjoyed the habit, and either way, in the bright light of awareness, do I enjoy it on my own?

For that matter, maybe everyone who finds themselves newly single, whether by death or divorce, should eventually sit down and answer the usual questions:

- Who am I? How would I describe myself to a stranger in 100 words?
- What reliably makes me laugh?
- What movies, music, books, etc. do I love, even if no one else does?

And so on.

Make it a date with yourself. Maybe have a glass of wine, maybe tea, whatever works. Enjoy it. Get to know the person who's always been there, apart from anyone else in your life. You've got the whole rest of your life to enjoy the relationship that comes of it.

Do It On Purpose

Nashville, TN
January 24, 2014.

Today I announced the closing of my company, [meta]marketer. I'm delighted with the positive and encouraging way the news has been received by friends, industry colleagues, the business community, and so on, and believe me I don't want to look that gift horse in the mouth. The message has largely been "times have changed and I'm shifting focus." And that's true, but here in my own corner of the digital world, I'd like to add a few brushstrokes of personal color to that story.

It starts with this: building and running a company is both harder and more rewarding than anyone has ever managed to convey to me. I'm sure I won't be the one to find the right words to get it across to you if you haven't experienced it. It challenged me on levels I never anticipated. But resolving my own internal issues around, say, what it means to lead with compassion and influence more often than authority left me a far better, stronger leader.

In fact the whole experience, from start to the impending finish, left me more aware of my flaws but more skilled at managing them, more wary of selling but more persuasive, more in touch with my limits as a communicator yet more in command of my range, and overall more sure of my capabilities and natural strengths.

"Freedom is what we do with what is done to us." — Jean-Paul Sartre

One of those natural strengths was made abundantly clear to me over the past few years in particular. When my husband died in mid-2012, it knocked the wind out of me personally and professionally. But as a business owner I had no choice but to get back to work as soon as I could manage it. Credit my team at the time: they came together, stepped up, and kept things running in the interim. Credit my close friends: they all but propped me up to keep me going. And with humility, credit me: I glued together every piece of resilience I had to come through the experience a whole, not a broken, person. I returned to work the following week. Sure, it was only for a few hours each day at first, but I went through the motions. And going through the motions is still forward motion.

Of course, even when I was physically back in the office for full days another week or two later, my focus and motivation was gutted. And it would be disingenuous not to admit that the company lost quite a bit of momentum in the fallout.

But I was determined not to let tragedy and grief cloud my decision of whether or not to keep the company going. For the remainder of 2012 and nearly all of 2013, I labored over what direction to go that would feel like a restart. I spent countless hours – some of it with my team, some of it with clients, past clients, and prospects, much of it alone or in conversations with close friends – sifting through opportunities, looking for a way forward that felt true.

* * *

So much good resulted from that. In the aftermath of devastating loss, my priorities and passions became much clearer to me. And what [meta]marketer had grown to be associated with was no longer where I wanted to invest my renewed energies.

On the other hand, some of the opportunities I've been afforded through the company's growth and profile – such as speaking at conferences and to various groups, writing for big audiences, mentoring and investing in startups, consulting with companies to solve strategic problems, and connecting with staggeringly amazing people all over the world – are exactly where I want to continue to invest those energies.

> "Above all, be the heroine of your life, not the victim."
> — Nora Ephron

I'm relieved that I got past the window when closing the company would have been a direct reaction to Karsten's death. I made as full a recovery at work as a person could wish for, and arrived at a decision based on a healthy perspective. Taking the time in 2013 to rebuild and reflect gave me the opportunity to really focus on my priorities and passions and to understand what's important to me.

Closing a company is a lot tougher decision than leaving a job. If I'm honest with you, it took me longer to make this decision than I might have preferred. And let me tell you, indecision is expensive. But that extra time did buy me confidence that I would be making the right decision.

And in the end, I've learned a lot about when and how to shed your old skin and emerge lighter, energized, and ready for new adventures.

> "Find out who you are and do it on purpose."
> — Dolly Parton

CHAPTER SEVEN
JOY, LAUGHTER, AND MEANING

Walking Through Woods

Nashville, TN
March 2014.

I took a walk through Radnor Lake today. It's a beautiful wooded area with a variety of walking and hiking trails. The last time I walked here with Karsten, the trees and the woods and the birds and the turtles and the deer and every little thing I saw reminded me of my dad. Now when I walk through here, those same trees and woods and birds and turtles and deer and every little thing remind me of Karsten.

In talking with people who have also survived the deaths of loved ones, and in particular those who seem to thrive afterward, it seems that a common theme is that the meaning of everything changes. The meaning of *everything* changes. Walking through the woods: new meaning. Drinking coffee in the morning: new meaning.

My impression is that this change occurs for everyone, or almost everyone, who suffers loss, but for some, the fact that everything has new meaning is overwhelming. That seems to be a big difference: whether the new meaning is ultimately welcome or not. Even if the death wasn't welcome, of course, ushering in the new meaning is not the same as welcoming the death. And the people who seem as if they're making that distinction also seem, in my admittedly unscholarly study of the subject, to be more likely to rebuild their lives well and thrive after loss.

The trick may well be to be intentional about meaning. Yes, drinking coffee in the morning will have new meaning. That may be hard. Maybe you had a cherished morning coffee ritual with the loved one who is gone. Maybe now you face a grief trigger every day just by waking up. So it might hurt every day for a while, or forever, that you no longer get to share that ritual. But somehow reclaiming that ritual and finding a way to make it your own is going to be part of the healing process.

Rituals can be an important part of healing from grief. And not just the public ones, like funerals. The private ones, like how many people visit graves to place flowers on them on certain days or for certain occasions, can be even more important to the healing process.

Beyond rituals, the rest of life as a whole seems to have new meaning. And the meaning of living with loss may not be appealing, but that's when I began to see the rest of my life as an undiscovered country. Which is what it is every day, but the heightened awareness loss brings casts bright light onto life's stage almost as if to say "what's next?" And that stage can look empty, especially when the figure who used to star in it is gone. But it's an opportunity to recast yourself as the lead, and determine where the story will go.

I did this by filling out a profile for an online dating site. Part of it was, sure, to meet people and test the waters, but part of doing it was an exercise: by filling out a form asking me to describe my interests, my taste in music and movies, my preferences for dining and entertainment, I was conscious about describing those answers without Karsten. He was such a profound influence on my tastes and my behaviors for fifteen years that it was tough work abstracting my own tastes and behaviors without him. Tough work, but meaningful and helpful work.

Getting clear about what matters to you is practically a gateway drug to creating a meaningful life. The process of sorting through my preferences and priorities, to assess whether they were my own or mine when I was partnered with Karsten, was foundational to understanding what might be next. People asked me right away when Karsten died if I was going to sell the house, move away, change jobs, and so on, and I couldn't quite comprehend why that was on people's minds. I think I understand that there's an impulse, sometimes, to make change like that in the immediate aftermath of loss, particularly tragic loss. But for me, I wanted to understand what I was doing first and why I would be making whatever decision I might make.

I found that I went back to the dating profile occasionally over a few weeks of thinking about it and refined my answers. I found that it was OK that there was still a bit of Karsten in the mix. He had been an influence on me for nearly a third of my life; there was bound to be some influence that had taken permanent hold. And for that I was grateful. But I was also grateful to find that I was beginning to know myself, and what mattered to me, in a new way.

The Awesomorial

Nashville, TN
March 14, 2014.

A month after Karsten died, he was due to have his first one-man art show in almost twenty years. So in starting to talk with friends about arrangements for a wake or funeral a day or so after he died, someone — it may have been me, but honestly I'm not sure — suggested we have the art show anyway as his memorial. If it was my idea, that was nearly the extent of my involvement. Friends picked it up and ran with it, infusing their own understanding of him into the planning, and what emerged was a multi-dimensional celebration of life that was bittersweet and darkly comic and honest and perfectly suited to his quirky character. He would never in a million years have wanted a dreary funeral. Funerals are for the living anyway.

When someone you love so much dies, it feels as if the pain revolves around you. It can take some readjustment to remember that there were countless other loved ones, friends, neighbors, and acquaintances who are sharing in the pain of loss. The art show / memorial seemed to be the perfect outlet for so many friends to express their love for this one-of-a-kind man.

So we didn't have a funeral for Karsten; we had an art show — his art, of course — and 'celebration of life' in a converted warehouse turned artists' collective and gallery. Everyone was encouraged to wear electric blue, which, after years of dying his soul patch blue, had become his signature color. Bulleit bourbon — his signature drink — was flowing freely on a sweltering night that turned out to be the hottest ever recorded in Nashville. It was over 100 degrees after sundown. The flow of air conditioning through the warehouse space was inconsistent, so the whole place felt like a sauna except for one spot under the industrial vent where people took turns under the icy blast of cold air. Something like 300 people showed up.

> "Life does not cease to be funny when people die any more than it ceases to be serious when people live." - George Bernard Shaw

So we were able to bring our collective memories of Karsten's playful spirit and creative vision together and, well, have a party. A friend later described it as having been "oddly awesome, for a memorial," and then merged the words to call it an "awesomorial."

I laughed a lot at Karsten's awesomorial. I heard beautiful stories about about my dear love, about how he listened and showed he cared, and hilarious stories about how he was the life of the party. I heard a few stories that were a little off-color, just as he would have liked. I couldn't imagine it going any other way. As one friend said, the only thing that felt wrong about that celebration of Karsten is that Karsten wasn't there, because it was totally his scene.

So Much Good, So Much Bad
* * *

Nashville, TN
    March 11, 2014.

A Vietnamese coworker of Karsten's used to say: so much good, so much bad.

I don't know what today holds; I only know that the last few days were full of joy for me and brought loss to quite a few of my friends. But I also know this: the sun will be shining today, and it will be warm and delightful, and there will be flowers and babies and new life to welcome, and there will be laughter if you permit it. There will be moments for grief, too, not that you'd be able to stop those moments if you tried. If today does bring you tears, maybe you can be grateful for the smiles that came before. And if today brings you smiles, I most definitely suggest being grateful for that.

My love to every one of you.

Suicide vs. Love

Nashville, TN
    August 16, 2014.

(Here's a hint: love wins.)

I'm supposed to be writing a book. I was supposed to write my regular column this week. There were a bunch of articles and blog posts I was scheduled to write, but all week I've been blocked. Truly. Couldn't write a thing. And now I realize it's because something I needed to write was blocking me. Isn't it funny: when people talk about "writers' block" the advice is rarely "well, write about what's blocking you, then." I tell you this to say: I had no intention of writing about this. Maybe ever. But I find that I have to in order to move on.

Robin Williams died, as everyone knows, this past Monday as I write this. That alone would have been a shock and cause for some sorrow. I was just enough of a fan of his comedy and some of his less-schmaltzy movies to feel some rare celebrity-death grief pangs. But because of the way he died, by suicide, and especially by asphyxiation, his death turned out to be a trigger for the grief of my own loss to suicide, my late husband Karsten.

If you aren't intimately acquainted with the idea of "triggers," let me explain. After a trauma — and certainly an unexpected death with a great deal of emotional complexity like suicide is a trauma — there are bound to be moments and events and emotional reactions and so on that somehow, suddenly, remind the traumatized brain of the initial trauma. It can feel like you're re-experiencing the whole thing. Only without the benefit of shock to soften the edges and dull the pain.

And even more difficult is how weird it sounds to admit to someone that you're in a bad state of mind because, y'know, Robin Williams died. It sounds like an overdramatic overreaction for someone who's not in any way connected to him. It's hard to explain that it's the parallel with my own loss that troubles me. It's hard to explain that it's not a ploy for attention. That's a kind of attention I have no desire for. It's a cyclical part of the complex grieving process that accompanies suicide. And what's more, to complete the cycle, Robin Williams' family and friends will probably experience these kinds of triggers, too, when people die from suicide, even people they don't know.

Part of what makes Robin Williams' death particularly challenging for suicide's survivors is how profuse the smell of ill-formed opinions became this week as everyone around the internet campfire weighed in with their take on it. I don't presume to say that many of the commentators hadn't experienced a close loss; it's a common enough phenomenon, sadly, that many if not most people have. But the level of reflection was dauntingly low about the circumstances that led to the loss, and about the circumstances of the lost one's life. The old cliches about suicide reared their heads. *But he was so funny!*

Karsten used to say that he could tell when things were bad for me because that's when I was at my funniest. I don't know if that's true; I think he was projecting a little of himself there. Karsten was funny, and

71

funny people see humor in everything, even the horrible stuff.

In a grief support community I'm part of, there's an effort to reclaim the language around suicide to make it less stigmatizing. Rather than say "he committed suicide," as is most common but which carries the connotation of a crime, people will soft-shoe the delivery with things like "he took his life," or "he ended his life." But some of the more activist-minded survivors advocate terminology like "he died by suicide" or the decidedly more weird-sounding noun-verb "he suicided."

The way language relates to the way we think is actually a pet topic of mine. I have no issue with coining neologisms as a tool in reframing discussion. So I agree that using terms that suggest less stigma is potentially a very good thing to make way for better mental health resources and so on.

It's just that none of these terms make me feel any more comfortable actually saying it.

Suicide is a tricky business. The organizations and charities related to it generally have one mission: to educate people, both those who might do the deed and those who might be in a position to help stop them, that suicide is preventable. I'm sure it is. I know there are many people, including dozens of friends of mine who've talked to me since Karsten's death, who have been close to the edge and who have, with help, walked away from it and don't envision ever returning to it. Most of us have probably found ourselves at one time or another close enough to the edge to crane our necks to see over from what, at least for me, was a safe enough distance not to trip and fall. But I know that I, for one, have never stood right at the edge, staring blankly into the abyss, reviewing all the reasons it was right for me, and delaying the jump only because of other people.

That's the thing. People talk about suicide as a "selfish" act. Of course in some ways it is; by doing it, you're robbing others of your presence and your future together, and people who are in that jagged mental state near the end never quite realize how much their presence is wanted and needed. And there are ripple effects and collateral damage from suicide that affect the survivors for the rest of their lives. But in another sense, we have to acknowledge that all the times people walk away from the edge to be with the ones they love and who love them are acts of unselfishness. I am convinced that the loving relationship that Karsten and I shared for nearly fifteen years was the thing that brought him back from the brink many, many times. Amidst the noisy chaos of anxiety and depression, with the amplification of insomnia, he still decided over and over again to walk back to life. His life with me. And I. AM. GRATEFUL. for that. That he ultimately couldn't make it work even longer does cause me intense sorrow, but I genuinely, legitimately feel gratitude for every time he must have decided that he could keep trying. I felt gratitude about that from the day he died. I think many times he stayed alive solely for me. It just didn't work that last time, and I feel deep, true anguish for him imagining how bleak his night must have been, making that final decision as I slept. My heart aches to imagine him making his plan, putting things in order, writing his note. And my imagination goes further, but I can't write about that. It approaches a level of some combined sacred and profane, and I don't have the writing skills or the emotional stamina to put words to it.

What I do know is this. I was never once angry with him, and I know I never will be. I don't think that saying this is the equivalent of a "get out of jail free" card to people who are suicidal; I just think compassion must tell us that many people walk away from the brink many times. And yes, this means we'd better be reaching out to people when they're on the brink. No doubt. Those suicide hotlines (1–800–273-TALK (8255) in the U.S.) and counselors are invaluable resources, and they certainly do a tough and necessary job. But the success rate there may well always be lower than 100%. Because there's a bigger job. It's not enough to love people when they're on the brink; we have to do the work of giving our love and compassion to the people we care about all the time.

As Karsten would say, we are self-aware primates, conscious of our place in the cosmic wonder. We're the only animal we know of that ponders the meaning of our existence. And as I say, all we have is the meaning we create for ourselves while we're here. We live for such a blip of time anyway. But our ability to love transcends the boundaries of life. We can carry love with us long after someone we love is gone, and we can give them that infinite sense of our love while they're here. Love doesn't die with death. Love is like liquid; when it pours out, it seeps into others' lives. Love changes form and shape. Love gets into everything. Death doesn't conquer all; love does. Love wins every single time. Love wins by lasting through death. Love wins by loving more, loving again, loving without fear.

That's the best I've got, after all of this. After life-changing love and loss, it comes down to this: love deeply. Love well. Love consistently. Love those closest to you, and love those you meet in passing. Show compassion. Feel empathy. Open your heart to the range of human emotion, and take your time with it. It's the best tool we have.

The love we give consistently just may be what someone recalls as they peer over the edge, and it may be the comfort they manage to bring themselves back to. Maybe then we have a chance at postponing someone's thoughts of suicide if we can't prevent them altogether. That's a start. And then maybe we have a chance of bringing that person some hope to balance their despair. Maybe we can help them not feel so alone on that precipice. Maybe we can meet them at the edge and walk them slowly back home, pausing every so often to hug and to notice the beautiful shape of the trees.

It's worth trying.

The Mattress Pattern

Nashville, TN
December 29, 2013.

Robbie asks me if I've flipped the bed. I haven't. I don't. It's not the thing I do; it's the thing he has taken to doing when we wash the sheets. He has a whole pattern of clockwise and upside-down turns to distribute the wear on the mattress as uniformly as possible. We have a growing set of these patterns and divisions of chores in our home life. I don't know where he is in the mattress pattern. There's a part of me that finds that a little discomforting, because I imagine being suddenly alone again and unable to ask which way the bed should be flipped.

It's not a rational thought, but it's one of the fleeting anxieties about not only being romantically involved with someone again, but spending real life together. I have not even finished processing all the legalities of Karsten's estate and our lives together and Robbie and I are now engaged. Should the unthinkable happen again, I imagine myself badly broken again and left processing more death bureaucracy than anyone should have to handle. And I worry about growing dependent on someone again in a way that I wouldn't know how to navigate aspects of my own life without him.

You think it's going to be the big milestone dates — the birthdays, the anniversaries, the day you first met — that overwhelm you with crippling grief. In September 2012, I was due to face three milestones in four days: the three-month mark since Karsten died, the anniversary of the day we met (which was the anniversary we'd always celebrated), and his birthday. In the middle of these, I had a ceremony to attend for an entrepreneurship award I was up for. I didn't want to go. At all. I had originally thought maybe I wanted to escape and go somewhere that week where I could disappear in a crowd. But then I thought I should be around friends. I was paralyzed with indecision. In fact, I was standing in the garden on our anniversary, the day before the event, half-staring at a flower and thinking about getting out of town for the rest of the week when my phone rang. It was a leader in the entrepreneur community, expressing his support and encouraging me to attend. I was moved, and called my friend Ashley who agreed to go with me. (I did win the award, by the way, and although Ashley's cheerleading as my name was called was sweet and selfless, it was still tough to be there without Karsten.)

But the truth is the milestones are never as hard in actuality as they are in anticipation. It's the dread of how bad they might be that's the worst. Living with the fear that you're going to end up unable to leave bed for days almost follows through as a self-fulfilling prophecy: the fear itself might keep you in bed, but the significant days themselves are rarely more sad than any other.

It turns out it's the little stuff that gets you. Most of the time what reduces you to a sobbing heap are petty details you can't believe you don't know, like which way the stupid mattress was last flipped.

Karsten always took care of the cats. I knew a little of how and when he fed the cats and cleaned the litter boxes. But what systems might he have had? What shortcuts? I had to devise my own. I'm pretty good at that kind of thinking anyway, but it was just one more thing, trivial though it seems, on top of a mountain of minutiae in our lives that I didn't know my way around. I didn't know what I needed to do to get my car registration renewed. I got pulled over for expired tags a few months after Karsten died. I told the officer my husband had just died and he was the one who did stuff like this and I hadn't figured out what I needed to do yet. Yep: I totally played the widow card. I was actually kind of hoping he'd explain what I needed to do. Nope: he totally wrote me a ticket. I still don't know what I probably ought to know about maintaining the house. But I learned how to clear a blocked drain, and damn it, I did it while hyper-conscious of the significance of my having to do it, choking back tears and grief. If I can do that, I'll figure out the rest.

And rationally I know that the dreaded worst-case-scenario outcome of losing Robbie isn't probable in the near future, and isn't the kind of concern I ought to have.

Perhaps there is something darkly romantic about the unspoken social idea that you die metaphorically when your love dies. At least that feels like a generous interpretation of why there seems to be such a prevalent and pervasive discomfort of seeking and finding happiness after loss.

I think there's a lot of guilt wrapped up in it, as if every time you laugh is a betrayal of your sadness. As if, if you fall in love again, you didn't love the lost love enough to last a lifetime.

But what that gothic idea overlooks is how much capacity you might now have to love. How being broken open makes light seep into all your darkest places. How you might have no choice but to love the world and embrace joy and seek meaning and find it, again and again and again. Cat litter and mattresses be damned.

CHAPTER EIGHT

MOVING THROUGH MILESTONES

Resurrection Lilies

Nashville, TN
   August 8, 2011.

My great aunt Marie was my father's mother's older sister, and the only great aunt I've ever really known. As kids, my sister and brother and I used to stay with her or with my grandparents in the retirement home where they lived whenever my parents took us to visit Baltimore, so we got to spend a fair bit of time getting to know her. She could be moody or reserved and sometimes strict with us kids, but she also had wit, warmth, a big cozy hug, and flashes of an attitude that hinted at the strong and funny younger woman she must have been.

Just as I was entering high school, Aunt Marie visited my parents' house in the Chicago suburbs and noticed some flowers growing in a patch of the yard untouched by the mower. You could see them from the screened-in back porch. My parents hadn't known what they were, but she recognized them as "resurrection lilies" — a flower she'd always loved as much for their name as their appearance. My dad, once he'd learned their name from his aunt, loved to sit on the back porch each August and point them out, reminding us that Aunt Marie was the one who identified them and how much she loved them.

Six years ago, when my dad was dying from cancer, the resurrection lilies came up and with help, he was just barely able to make it to the back porch for one last viewing of the resurrection lilies. Once again, he reminded us about how Aunt Marie loved those flowers. As I helped him back to bed, he told me that after he died, he wanted me to dig up some of those lilies and plant them in my garden in Nashville, which he never had a chance to see, in memory of Aunt Marie and him.

My dad died November 5th of that year, and even early November in the Chicago area is usually ridiculously cold. That year was no exception. After the day had quieted down a bit, I went out back to where they were planted. The ground was hard from the cold but the digging felt good and cathartic, and eventually I managed to dig up three good bulbs.

I put them in a plastic bag in my parents' refrigerator to bring home with me a few days later. It was cold when I got back to Nashville, so I worried about putting them right into the ground, which meant that they stayed in our refrigerator until the next spring, when one day I happened to notice a little bit of green emerging from the bulbs right inside the baggie in the fridge.

So I got outside and placed them in a line of three and planted a semicircle of daylilies around them to accent them. And they continued to sprout leaves, which died back as they're supposed to, but no flowers ever emerged that summer.

I was a little worried they weren't very healthy after their difficult transition, but the following spring the leaves came up again and I got hopeful that they might actually flower that year.

And then in late July, there they were, beautiful as can be.

The resurrection lilies blooming in my garden

They skip a year now and then but come up occasionally to remind me of my dad and his aunt. They grow incredibly fast — sometimes they're over two feet high before I've even noticed them coming up.

I write all of this because a few days ago, my niece Cole gave birth to her first child: my great nephew Sammy. Which makes me a great aunt. And now that I am, I can't help feeling like those fast-growing, resurrecting, surviving flowers are my connection with my Great Aunt Marie and my dad in welcoming Sammy to the family and to the world, and recognizing that life does, after all, go on.

Dates and Numbers

Nashville, TN
September 28, 2013.

My mind has always been mildly obsessed with numbers. Words, too, but in a different way. You know that scene in "A Beautiful Mind" when John Nash, played by Russell Crowe, is looking at the coded numbers on the wall and pulling patterns from them?

Well, my mind is nothing like that. I mean it is, but it's nowhere near that useful. It puzzles over numbers until it finds patterns, but in a far less amazing way. I'm not so good with spatial stuff or visualizing abstract imagery, but gimme a bunch of numbers and I'll make connections between 'em all day long. Associate words or some kind of meaning with them, which is fundamentally what happens with dates, and they're in my head forever.

So it's probably no surprise that anniversaries and calendar milestones stick with me. Not all of them, of course, but the ones I've somehow deemed significant carry such weight that I can feel their impending arrival days or even weeks ahead of time.

November 5th: when my dad died. June 25th: when Karsten died. And the September double-whammy week: September 26th and 28th, the date on which I met Karsten, and his birthday, respectively. Hardly anyone knew the exact date of Karsten's birthday because he didn't like to make a big deal of it, but of course I knew. One of my favorite memories over the last few years was when our happy hour group staged a surprise blue-soul-patch celebration in the vague timeframe of his 50th birthday since I wouldn't tell anyone specifically what date it was, only that it was coming up.

Les and Freeman sporting blue soul patches with Karsten (at right) at Karsten's 50th close-enough-to-birthday party

But the thing about the calendar is it's a fixed repeating framework for measuring time, whereas time itself goes on indefinitely. So every year, every date accumulates meaning. Those dates will probably never NOT mean those things to me, but as years go by they will also take on new meaning as new things happen on them.

Which means that every date has the potential for all kinds of associations, with all kinds of feelings. All at once, potentially.

Since I've been writing a book about loss and moving forward, I've been trying to put into useful words how it works, this pattern of triggers and reminiscences while creating new meaning. I've been a widow for over a year and a quarter. And for darn near all of 2013, I've been in a wonderful relationship with Robbie, a man I fell for hard and fast and am now engaged to. December 18th: the day of the photo shoot that brought us together. February 2nd: the date of the party that clinched it all for us.

But the calendar repeats and repeats, and the timeline of my many previous stories and significant dates will continue to weave through the timeline of my ongoing stories and dates. Grief isn't a gradual fade; it's spiky. It comes in bursts with triggers like sights and sounds and words and numbers. And for many of us, especially dates.

It isn't strange at all, to me, that I am living from a place of genuine delight and happiness, and also feeling pangs of grief when the numbers line up in a certain way. If you'll forgive me the hokey rhyme, the healing is in what you do with the feeling.

So here's what I want do with this feeling, today: since Karsten isn't here for me to wish happy birthday to, I would very much like to wish all my friends a happy day. I wish you inspiration and enlightenment, and a day full of creativity, curiosity, and great conversation, and, of course, a night full of partyin' like a rockstar. And love, love, love all you can while you can. Life is short and sometimes hard, but love is like renewable energy. And the calendar is only a counting tool; it can't stop time from moving forward and creating new meaning, and it shouldn't keep you from doing so either.

Thanks, Josh Ritter, For Getting Me Ready For Monday

Nashville, TN
November 3rd, 2007.

Monday is the anniversary of my dad's death, again. It was a reflective time for me last year and it's looking like it will be the same this year.

I can tell because last night we went to see Josh Ritter. There was a song he played with lyrics that said "tell me I got here at the right time" and it was bittersweet and melancholy and painted a picture of loving someone through illness, and it got me thinking about the process of caring for my dad while he was sick and the acceptance I had to come to about the possibility that in one of my trips back to Nashville, I would not be there when he died. And that's basically how it worked out in the end — Karsten and I had just made it back to Chicago that evening and decided not to go by my parents' house until the next morning since it was already pretty late. And my dad died that night.

83

Sometimes the loss hurts more because I know I could have seen him alive one more time, but more often I know I was there at the right times all the previous times.

Anyway, it's funny how once you're reminded of something difficult, you can see connections in the loosest ways. So all through the rest of Josh Ritter's set, I was primed to reflect on all kinds of loss, but especially my dad. And then he played "Kathleen," which is one of the few songs of his I knew before last night, and I like it but it's a tough one for me, because it so heavily references the Irish standard "I'll Take You Home Again, Kathleen" — one of the songs my dad used to sing when he was a nightclub performer and the origin of my given name. Of course, Ritter's song goes off in a different direction, but I think if you carry the connection over and think about his song in the context of its heritage, it makes his song even more intriguing. The Irish song is a plea to that song's Kathleen to hold out hope in the narrator, to recognize that he sees she is unhappy and that he can once again bring her the happiness that she has lost. The Ritter song is a plea to its Kathleen to place some hope in the narrator, to recognize that he appreciates her and can see her clearly and can make her happy even if it's just for one night. Each song is a kind of begging, but from nearly opposite ends of the lifecycle of a relationship — and, you could even say, nearly opposite ends of life itself.

Anyway, I thought about that while he was playing the song, but I was also just washed away by the bittersweet significance every time I heard the line "I'll be the one to drive you home, Kathleen."

Forgetting About Father's Day

Nashville, TN
June 17th, 2007.

I wonder about the organizers of Bonnaroo, and whether they intentionally scheduled the festival for the weekend of Father's Day. You have to figure that with 80,000 some attendees, there are bound to be a whole lot of arguments about missing the family cookout or whatever.

As I am not attending Bonnaroo nor is my father living nor am I within proximity of any kind of family cookout, I have no such dilemma. My dilemma pertains more to simply getting through Father's Day with the least amount of psychological trauma.

Here, in no particular order, are a few ideas that have occurred to me thus far:

Stay in bed.
Tempting. On the other hand, Karsten points out that it will be there all day. I can always keep it as a fall-back option.

Go for a walk in a park or other natural space.
Good possibility. It's especially meaningful if there are a lot of birds around, since my dad used to love to watch the birds. But it might be too hot for this to be a pleasant experience, so I'll have to wait and see how the day shapes up.

Sit on the front steps and try to enjoy the beautiful day.
Already getting a jump on this one. Sitting out here with my laptop and a pot of coffee. But again, in an hour or so, it will probably warm up to where this won't be pleasant anymore.

Do day-job work.
Yeah, no.

Write a song or three.
Very probable. I did a little last night and was surprised at some of what came out.

Clean, tidy, organize.
I'll see how I feel. This would be helpful to do, but I just don't feel motivated to do it.

Organize files on my computer.
Same as above.

* * *

Plan my upcoming party.

I need to do this, and it might be fun. So maybe this will be a good stay-inside-while-it's-hot activity.

Go back to bed.

I know, I already talked about bed. But it's sounding like such an appealing option.

I do genuinely wish a happy Father's Day to anyone out there to whom it applies. And I genuinely wish good alternatives for anyone who needs them.

One Small Year and Some Tiny Kittens

Nashville, TN
November 5, 2006.

"One small year
It's been an eternity
It's taken all of me to get here"
- One Small Year - Shawn Colvin

Well, here it is: the day I've been dreading. It's been one year since my dad died. I thought I would have a lot to say about that, but I find myself oddly quiet on the subject. I did write an email to my sister this morning, and said this:

> I still miss Dad very much, of course, but I'm also amazed at how
> much healing happens in the course of one year. Then again, I'm
> equally amazed at how much still hurts after a whole year has passed.
> It's almost like time and healing can be measured in two different
> dimensions, on two different scales, with one exceeding my
> expectations and one falling so very short. Or whatever. I guess that's

why it's easier just to say "life is funny." ;)

Yesterday, the Race for the Cure came through our neighborhood, and I stood outside with a cup of coffee and watched them, thinking of my dad who used to enjoy running, and how he lost his race. But it was encouraging to see how many people turned out to help raise money for the cause. Maybe cancer will someday be a thing of the past.

Speaking of raising money for good causes, last night, we went to two fundraisers. The first was for the Nashville Humane Association: Anipalooza. Heh. We went to the one last year, too, and I'm sorry to say that this year's wasn't as good as last year's. Last year they had doggie speed dating, which was just about the cutest thing ever, but that was gone this year for whatever reason. The music in the main tent was also too loud, meaning you could barely hear someone shouting next to you, and you sure weren't going to casually mix and mingle and get to know new people.

On the plus side, there were kittens inside the shelter, which just about makes up for any shortcoming in event planning. Just like last year, Karsten was in one of the cat rooms playing with kittens most of the time we were there, and drew a crowd watching him get the kittens all excited. You should have seen these kittens crawling all over Karsten. I took pictures but they only hint at the stinging cuteness of it all.

After that, we went to back to our neighborhood for the "Heart and Soul" benefit at Werthan Lofts, for the American Heart Association. The contrast was stunning: someone there must actually be a professional event planner. They gave out wine glasses to each attendee, along with maps of the building showing the lofts that were open for the event. And then they had signs up on the hallway walls and balloons marking the entrance of each open unit to help people find their way through the somewhat confusing layout of the building. Plenty of volunteers, plenty of wine, plenty of cool people, and plenty of music ensured that it was a great party. A lot of folks were there from the Germantown neighborhood, too, which was fun.

A Vietnamese coworker of Karsten's used to say: so much good, so much bad. I think of that a lot, and I consider it a victory when the bad doesn't overshadow the good. Right now, as much as it still hurts to miss my dad, I know the good in my life — like loving and being loved so deeply by someone as wonderful as Karsten, and having a job I enjoy, and being part of a community of great people, and living in a home we have the ability to enjoy and improve, and having good friends, not to mention that I was lucky enough to have had a dad as wonderful as he was — all that good is as bright as sunlight and nothing can overshadow it. And I guess that should be enough to get me through another small year.

Surviving the First Year

Nashville, TN
  June 24, 2013.

Tomorrow, June 25th, it will have been one year since Karsten died.

I've gained a vast amount of insight about life in the last year. I learned that the initial year after you lose someone is sometimes called "the year of firsts," because every experience, no matter how mundane, becomes significant when it's the first time you're doing it without your loved one.

***

Karsten and me, December 2005, photo credit Joe Hendricks

I learned that there are a lot of aspects to what it means to pick up and carry on after someone you love dies. There are the practical matters, the earthly things. None of these is simple to deal with, although some are more complicated than others. After I got over the initial resistance to sorting through Karsten's clothes and shoes, it was relatively easy very early on to give away or box most of them up, yet despite several attempts, I have yet to make much of a dent in going through his collected treasures, art supplies, reference works, and the plastic filing tubs with folders stuffed with concept sketches in his art studio.

There are the issues of time and habit and what we used to do together, and what he used to do for me and for us. He used to carry things for me as a matter of routine, always saying "beautiful hands shouldn't have to lift heavy things." I remembered with sadness his saying that as I carried grocery bags up the front stairs by myself the first few times, but after a few months, that chore had already become commonplace.

Some things are mundane but important, like various kinds of household maintenance, for which I've had to find substitute arrangements, like hiring a lawn service, or for which I've had to learn new skills, like clearing a blocked drain. Some things are routine and important, so I've had to develop new habits and modify my schedule around feeding the cats and cleaning the litter boxes. Some less mundane things I've learned to do without, like taking evening walks around the neighborhood. I tried to do those alone for a while, but it just didn't feel right without him.

And then there's the issue of companionship, of romance, of love. It may sound surprising, but I dipped my toe back into the dating pool less than two months after Karsten died. I'm a quick study, both intellectually and emotionally; I'd already done a lot of the work of grieving and processing my new reality by then, and I felt like I needed to laugh and find some joy. People so often tell such horror stories about dating; I wasn't sure what to expect. I was incredibly lucky to have a series of mostly charming experiences over the next several months with a cast of enjoyable characters. I sought out people with funny stories to tell, and I heard enough tales to fill a few books. (And yes, I kept notes.) Those months of dating helped me feel stronger, more discerning, and more sure of my own identity, independent of the me that had been dissolved and conjoined into happy couplehood for the past fifteen years, the me that suddenly felt shockingly naked and incomplete when the other half of that couple was unexpectedly gone.

All of which meant that after those first few months of dating, I was feeling steady on my feet when the real thing began to happen organically — a work-related photo shoot unexpectedly yielded a dinner date and then turned into a magical evening at an impersonator party and then into spending lots of time together and then into spending as little time apart as possible — and by then I was sure enough of myself to let it grow at its own pace and into its own thing without concern for whether I was ready.

You don't always know when you learn something how and when it's going to be useful to you. One of the most valuable pieces of wisdom I've ever heard came from my friend Lee years ago, quoting Neil Gaiman, who said "the difference between comedy and tragedy is where you stop telling the story." It's made this past year so much easier. Life goes on; you live, you learn; for every bad, there is good; seek the whole truth. Be grateful, be grateful, be grateful.

I'd like to share with you some of what I've learned in this year, in no particular order:

- As someone who values self-sufficiency and not being a burden on others, when situations force you to lean on friends, it can be a pretty jarring experience. But without the ability to accept help, you don't know true humility. And without knowing how to ask for help, you don't know the intimacy of trusting your friends. They're both skills worth learning and experiences worth having.

- No one knows what to say, and what some people think is appropriate can be upsetting at best, and devastating at worst. But empathy for the fact that people are doing the best they know to do, along with patience and grace, can smooth over a lot of awkwardness.

- My grief is not the only grief. Some people grieve by being angry. Some grieve by telling all their funniest stories. I have seen a wide range of reactions, and none is right or wrong. I feel for everyone who lost Karsten, and I recognize that I am their closest link to him. The way his and our friends interacted with me was often more of a reflection of their grief for him than their feelings about me.

- When the unthinkable happens, your horizon shatters and everything in your worldview becomes fractured. It can be impossible to handle day-to-day activities with appropriate perspective. But recovery is a long process of reassembling the fragments. There's a balance to strike between challenging yourself to go back to work, be social, and move forward, and allowing yourself the safety of escape and avoidance to recover and heal in private or with very close friends.

♦ And here's an extra hint about that: the right balance changes all the time. There's no substitute for listening to your instinct. If you feel like you might need to skip a social event, then you just might need to skip that social event. But if you cut yourself too much slack and don't risk a few awkward meetings, you make no progress.

♦ As is true in evolutionary biology, to survive catastrophic change, you must adapt. But adapting and surviving describes a merely functional level of existence; there is an opportunity to thrive, but it means seeing the remainder of your life as an undiscovered country, a place full of wonder and unknown experiences. You have to embrace the opportunity your new reality grants you. And you must reinvent yourself to match it.

♦ I think the reason this is difficult is because of guilt. To thrive and enjoy life after someone we love dies at some level seems to imply that their loss meant nothing, or that adjusting to their absence was easy. But I think this has something to do with our social taboo about death. If we accept that death is a part of life, we can perhaps think of our lives as timelines that overlap each other but don't start and end together. When one person's timeline ends before ours does, we have the luxury of continuing to live and we are all but obligated to do so.

So here's to marking the end of the "year of firsts." Here's to learning humility and accepting help from friends. Here's to loving again. Here's to surviving death. Here's to life. Onward.

Kate O'Neill is a writer, speaker, and observer of meaningful experiences. She is founder and CEO of KO Insights, which offers training and guidance for customer-centric strategic marketing. Her prior roles include owning and running digital strategy and analytics firm [meta]marketer, creating the first content management role at Netflix, developing Toshiba America's first intranet, and holding leadership positions in a variety of digital content and technology start-ups. She writes regularly for The Tennessean, contributes to CMO.com and a variety of other publications, and is the author of an upcoming book on meaningfulness in marketing.

Kate has been featured in CNN Money, TIME, Forbes, USA Today, and other national media, and has been named "Technology Entrepreneur of the Year," "Social Media Strategist of the Year," a "Power Leader in Technology" and a "Woman of Influence," along with numerous other awards and recognitions.

More information about Kate, including ways to connect, can be found at:

http://www.koinsights.com/about/about-kate-oneill/